# SINGLE SPIES

*Two plays about*
*Guy Burgess and Anthony Blunt*

## &

# TALKING HEADS

*Six Monologues*

*by*

## ALAN BENNETT

SUMMIT BOOKS

NEW YORK · LONDON · TORONTO
SYDNEY · TOKYO · SINGAPORE

SUMMIT BOOKS
Simon & Schuster Building
Rockefeller Center
1230 Avenue of the Americas
New York, New York l0020

First Summit Books Edition 1990
Published by arrangement with the author
SINGLE SPIES originally published in Great Britain
by BBC Books
TALKING HEADS originally published in Great Britain
by Faber and Faber Limited
SUMMIT BOOKS and colophon are trademarks
of Simon & Schuster Inc.
Designed by Edith Fowler
Manufactured in the United States of America

10 9 8 7 6 5 4 3 2 1

Library of Congress Cataloging in Publication Data

Bennett, Alan.
    Single spies : two plays about Guy Burgess and
Anthony Blunt ; & Talking heads : six monologues /
by Alan Bennett.—1st Summit Books ed.
        p.  cm.
    Contents: Single spies: An Englishman abroad.
A question of attribution—Talking heads: A chip in
the sugar. Bed among the lentils. A lady of letters.
Her big chance. Soldiering on. A cream cracker
under the settee.
    1. Burgess, Guy, 1911–1963—Drama.
    2. Blunt, Anthony, 1907–1983—Drama.
    I. Bennett, Alan, 1934–  Talking heads.
1990.
    II. Title.
PR6052.E5S56    1990                    90–9423
822'.914dc20                                CIP
ISBN 0–671–69249–6

# Foreword

THIS BOOK brings together my television series, *Talking Heads*, first shown on the BBC in 1988, and *Single Spies*, two one-act plays that opened as a double bill at the National Theatre in 1988 and in the West End the following year. The two halves of the book are very different, and though the writer is not the best judge, reading them I would find it hard to say that they were by the same person. This may not need justifying, but it does need explaining.

I was born and brought up in Leeds in the north of England, where my father was a butcher. As a boy, I sometimes went out on the bike, delivering orders to customers, including a lady called Mrs Fletcher. Mrs Fletcher had a daughter, Valerie, who went to Leeds Girls High School and to secretarial college, and then on to London where she got a job with a publishing firm. She did well there and eventually became secretary to one of the directors, whom, though he was much older than she was, she eventually married. The firm was Faber and Faber, and the director was T. S. Eliot. So there was a time when I thought my only connection with literature would be that I had once delivered meat to T. S. Eliot's mother-in-law.

A few years later when I was about to go to university, my mother came in one day and said, 'I ran into Mrs Fletcher down the road. She wasn't with Mr Fletcher. She was with another feller, tall, elderly, very refined looking. She introduced me, and we passed the time of day'. It wasn't until some time later that I realised that, without it being one of the most momentous encounters in western literature, my mother had met T. S. Eliot. I tried to explain to her the significance of the great poet but without much success, *The Waste Land* not figuring very largely in my mother's scheme of things. 'The thing is', I said finally, 'he won the Nobel Prize'. 'Well', she said with that unerring grasp of inessentials which is the prerogative of mothers, 'I'm not surprised. It was a beautiful overcoat'.

Other than this second-hand glimpse of the great poet, there was nothing of literary interest in my childhood, but the point of the story for me is that it does illustrate, if it does not explain why, when I came to write it should be in two such different voices. Because if one takes T. S. Eliot to represent Art, Culture and Literature, all of them, including Class, very much in the upper case, and my mother, resolutely in the lower case, to represent life, then what happened on that suburban street corner was what is happening thirty years later between the covers of this book.

It wasn't that I had any particular affection for the works of T. S. Eliot. I had seen, though not entirely understood, *The Cocktail Party* when it came to the Leeds Grand Theatre on its pre-London tour, and *Murder in the Cathedral* done at a local church. I had even read *Notes Towards a Definition of Culture*, but only because I was soon to take a scholarship examination and it seemed the kind of thing one was expected to read. And just as one read what one was expected to read, so when one started very haltingly to write, one wrote what one was expected to write . . . not, that is, about life, in my case the life of a northern town, provincial, unmetropolitan, dull and, at that time, in the late 1950s, largely unwritten about, but the life, metropolitan, middle class, that I had read about in books or seen at Saturday matinees at the Grand Theatre. Admittedly these first efforts only took the form of sketches and parodies, which I performed at concerts at Oxford, but they led in 1960 to writing and performing in the revue *Beyond the Fringe*. My first stage play, *Forty Years On* (1968), was set in a private school (I had gone to a state school); it was peopled with characters like Virginia Woolf and Cyril Connolly whom I had read about (rather than read) and was an elegy for an upper-class England that through background and education I had never known. And though they were written twenty years later, it's to that world that the two plays that compose *Single Spies* belong. In the meantime, though, I had begun to write television plays that did draw on my own background and experience, my characters at last beginning to speak in a voice that was, and is, like my own, and which speaks in *Talking Heads*.

Of course, as a literary apprenticeship, mine isn't particularly unusual. Art comes out of art; it begins with imitation, often in the form of parody. It's in the process of imitating the voices of others that one comes to learn the sound of one's own. But with me, the process has been arrested, the fissure persists, T. S. Eliot and my mother never really joining hands. I still have the voice I was born with and the one I acquired.

Oddly, though, my first effort to speak in a voice that was my own rather than putting one on happened in New York. *Beyond the Fringe* played on Broadway from October 1962 to April 1964, and towards the end of 1963, the show was revamped and with some new sketches went into a second edition. I chose to do a monologue about death and, in particular, death and its supposedly comic aspects in the north of England. Now death in 1963 was not the subject of lively interest it has since become, and even today it's hardly big on Broadway. This was also death in a north of England setting, which was not one Broadway audiences could be expected to know about or to want to. I performed the sketch nightly for six months to the embarrassment of my colleagues and the mystified silence of the audience, and when the revue ended it was nearly ten years before I ventured to write about the north of England again. The first round had gone to T. S. Eliot.

ALAN BENNETT<br>
London, 1989

# SINGLE SPIES

# Contents

# Introduction

SOME YEARS AGO a stage play of mine, *The Old Country*, was running in the West End. The central character, Hilary, played by Alec Guinness, was a Foreign Office defector living in Russia. Hilary was generally identified as Philby, though that had not been my intention, the character having much more in common with a different sort of exile, W. H. Auden. However, during the run of *The Old Country*, friends and well-wishers would come round after the performance, often with reminiscences of Philby and his predecessors, Burgess and Maclean. One of these was Coral Browne who told me of her visit to Russia with the Shakespeare Memorial Theatre in 1958 and the particular incidents that make up *An Englishman Abroad*.

The picture of the elegant actress and the seedy exile sitting in a dingy Moscow flat through a long afternoon listening again and again to Jack Buchanan singing 'Who stole my heart away'? seemed to me funny and sad but it was a few years before I got round to writing it up. It was only when I sent Coral Browne the first draft of the television film that I found she had kept not merely Burgess's letters, thanking her for running his errands, but also her original notes of his measurements and even his cheque (uncashed and for £6) to treat her and one of her fellow actors to lunch at the Caprice. The original script of the television film was quite close to the version now presented on the stage. It had no exterior shots because I knew no BBC budget would run to filming in Moscow or some foreign substitute. I introduced the exteriors only when a suitable (and a suitably economic) substitute for Moscow was found in Dundee.

I have put some of my own sentiments into Burgess's mouth. 'I can say I love London. I can say I love England. I can't say I love my country, because I don't know what that means' is a fair statement of my own, and I imagine many people's, position. The Falklands War helped me to understand how a fastidious stepping-aside from

11

patriotism could be an element in characters as different as Blunt and Burgess. Certainly in the spy fever that followed the unmasking of Professor Blunt I felt more sympathy with the hunted than the hunters.

I never met Blunt, but though he seems to have been an altogether less likeable character than Burgess he is a more familiar type, at any rate in academic circles. Championed by his pupils he was less favourably regarded by some of his colleagues, who found him arrogant and opinionated. There are plenty of dons like this, in whom shyness, self-assurance and deep conviction combine to give an uncongenial impression. Housman and Wittgenstein are perhaps the most distinguished examples. In death such characters are invariably filed under the obituarist's catch-all 'Did not suffer fools gladly'.

In the first play it is suggested that Burgess was a spy because he wanted a place where he was alone, and that having a secret supplies this. I believe this to be psychologically true, but there is a sense too that an ironic attitude towards one's country and a scepticism about one's heritage is a part of that heritage. And so, by extension, is the decision to betray it. It is irony activated.

I find it hard to drum up any patriotic indignation over either Burgess or Blunt, or even Philby. No one has ever shown that Burgess did much harm, except to make fools of people in high places. Because he made jokes, scenes and, most of all, passes, the general consensus is that he was rather silly. Blunt was not silly and there have been attempts to show that his activities had more far-reaching consequences, but again he seems to be condemned as much out of pique and because he fooled the Establishment as for anything that he did. It is Philby who is always thought to be the most congenial figure. Clubbable, able to hold his liquor, a good man in a tight corner, he commends himself to his fellow journalists, who have given him a good press. But of all the Cambridge spies he is the only one of whom it can be proved without doubt that he handed over agents to torture and death.

I think it's about time we stopped thinking of treachery as the crime of crimes. It suits governments to make it so and the sentences handed down by judges reflect this. But the world is a much smaller place nowadays. At the height of the Cold War Maclean's understanding of Western scruples is said to have had a moderating effect on Soviet policy and the message seems to be that the more we know about each other the less dangerous the world is likely to be. Moral indignation seems beside the point. To conceal information is always more respectable than to reveal it but are governments and prime ministers who hush up evidence of nuclear accidents, as Macmillan is now known to have done in 1957, less culpable than our Cambridge villains? Of course Blunt, Burgess and Co. had the advantage of us in that they still had illusions. The trouble with treachery nowadays is that if one does want to betray one's country there is no one satisfactory to betray it to. If there were, more people would be doing it.

*Single Spies*, a double bill of *An Englishman Abroad* and *A Question of Attribution*, was first performed at the Lyttelton Theatre, South Bank, London, on 1 December 1988. The cast was as follows:

A N  E NGLISHMAN  A BROAD

| | |
|---|---|
| CORAL | Prunella Scales |
| BURGESS | Simon Callow |
| TOLYA | Paul Brightwell |
| TAILOR | Alan Bennett |
| SHOP ASSISTANT | Edward Halsted |
| | |
| *Director* | Alan Bennett |
| *Designer* | Bruno Santini |
| *Lighting* | Paul Pyant |

A  Q UESTION OF  A TTRIBUTION

| | |
|---|---|
| BLUNT | Alan Bennett |
| RESTORER | David Terence |
| CHUBB | Simon Callow |
| PHILLIPS | Crispin Redman |
| COLIN | Brett Fancy |
| HMQ | Prunella Scales |
| | |
| *Director* | Simon Callow |
| *Designer* | Bruno Santini |
| *Lighting* | Paul Pyant |
| *Music* | Dominic Muldowney |

*An Englishman Abroad*

CHARACTERS

BURGESS

CORAL

TOLYA

TAILOR

SHOP ASSISTANT

# An Englishman Abroad

*A projection screen hides the set. Stage right of the screen is
a bentwood chair. The screen glows red and projected on it
is the head of Stalin as we hear a record of Jack Buchanan
singing 'Who stole my heart away'?*

*The song fades as* CORAL BROWNE *enters stage right.
She is a striking woman, tall and elegant, and carrying a
luxurious fur coat.*

CORAL:    Stalin died in 1953. I was in *Affairs of State* at the time, a
light comedy that had a decent run at the Cambridge. Stalin had had
a decent run too, though I'd never been a fan of the old boy, even
during the war when he was all the rage. It wasn't so much the cult of
personality that put me off (being in the theatre I'm no stranger to
that); it was the moustache. One smiles, but more judgements than
people care to admit are grounded in such trivialities, and when
you're just a fool of an actress like me you don't mind coming out
with it.

After Uncle Joe's death they played with the understudies for a bit,
then brought in a cast of unknowns in something called *The Thaw*.
Soviet experts in the West (what nowadays would be called 'experi-
enced Kremlin-watchers') thought that this show was going to run
and run, predicting—poor loves—that the Iron Curtain was about to
go up and stay up. Ah well. Incidentally, don't let any of this deceive
you into thinking I took any sort of interest in Soviet affairs. Actresses
are excused newspapers much as delicate boys used to be excused
games; the only paper I see regularly is *The Stage*, and its coverage of
the comings and goings in the Politburo is to say the least, cursory.

Still, there were repercussions, even on me. When peace breaks
out suddenly, as it did then, culture is first on the menu, actors and
musicians sent in ahead of the statesmen like the infantry before the
tanks. We had the Red Army Choir; they got the Stratford Memorial

Theatre in *Hamlet*. Michael Redgrave was the eponymous prince, and notwithstanding I was scarcely five minutes older than he was, I played his mother.

> (GUY BURGESS *enters stage left. He is in his early fifties, a man who has once been handsome but is now running to seed.*)

BURGESS:   Hearing that Stalin had died one cheered up no end. It wasn't just that I was glad to see the back of the old bugger, though I was, but for the first time since I'd come to Moscow in 1951 I found I'd something to do. Death always means work for somebody, and one was suddenly very busy reading the papers, monitoring news broadcasts, collating and analysing Western reactions to the Marshal's somewhat overdue departure. However, in no time at all, they had him tucked in beside Lenin on Red Square, and life returned to what I had come to regard as normal. Doing *The Times* crossword, the *Statesman* competition, reading Trollope and Jane Austen. A gentleman of leisure. Of course, the most accomplished exiles are and always have been the Russians. They're tutors in it practically. So, in a sense, we had come to the right place.

What made it harder to bear was that no one in what one couldn't help thinking of as the outside world actually knew we were here. For the first few years of our sojourn we were kept very much under wraps—no letters, no phone calls, nothing. It made Greta Garbo look gregarious. I say 'we', meaning my colleague Maclean, with some diffidence. It's dispiriting to find oneself yoked permanently to someone who was never meant to be more than a travelling companion (besides having been a fellow travelling companion, of course). Now it was 'we', handcuffed together in the same personal pronoun.

Quarantine or honeymoon, our period of probation ended when we were revealed to the world's press in Moscow in 1956. After that, though we never exactly hit the cocktail party circuit and still had to mind our ps and qs, there was less—shall we say—skulking. (BURGESS *exits left.*)

CORAL:   Dissolve to my dressing-room in the Moscow Art Theatre one night after the performance. I am sitting there, applying the paint-stripper, when I hear a commotion next door. Suddenly Hamlet bursts in. Someone is being sick in his dressing room, would I assist?

Now vomiting is not childbirth. If one is having a baby a helping hand is not unwelcome. If one is having a puke, one is best left alone to get on with it. Remembering always that nausea requires patience. One of the few lessons I have learned in life is that when one is sick it is always in threes. Judging by the state of the carpet this was a lesson this particular gentleman had yet to learn. When his face came out of the basin I found I knew it, though not by name. The moment for introductions was long since past and Redgrave did not make them. I cleaned the man up, noting that he was English, he was upper class, and he was drunk. It was only later that night when a note was slipped under my door at the hotel that I found out he was also Guy Burgess. (CORAL *has put on her fur coat and she takes a note from the pocket.*) 'Bring a tape measure'. Bring a tape measure?

> (*The motif of Stalin has faded from the screen and as we hear* BURGESS *singing the screen rises to reveal his very untidy flat. There is an easy chair, a sofa and a small table, several bookshelves filled to overflowing with books and papers (the books plainly English) and at the rear of the flat a kitchenette. Through an alcove is a double bed, unmade and the sheets unwashed, and stage left is a pianola.*)

BURGESS:   (*Singing off*)
> Oh God our help in ages past
> Our hope for years to come,
> Our shelter from the stormy blast
> And our eternal home.

(BURGESS *wanders in, shaving.*)

> Before the hills in order stood
> Or earth received her frame

(*The doorbell rings.*)

> From everlasting Thou art God,
> It's open.
> Through endless years the same.

(BURGESS *hurriedly clears some dirty clothes from a chair and as an afterthought flings the heaped contents of an ashtray under the sofa, as* CORAL *enters through the hallway stage right.*)

BURGESS:   *(To* CORAL) Hello.

CORAL:   *(Puffed)* The stairs!

BURGESS:   I know. I'm sorry. Recover. What a splendid coat. Let me take it. *(He buries his face in the grand fur coat before dropping it, pretty unceremoniously, on the sofa.)*

BURGESS:   Mmm. Have a drink.

CORAL:   Please.

BURGESS:   I've just been tidying up. *(He sweeps some stuff to the floor and removes his soap and towel.)*

CORAL:   One moment. My soap. This is my soap.

BURGESS:   It is. It is. Palmolive: for that schoolgirl complexion.

CORAL:   So it was you who took my cigarettes?

BURGESS:   One wasn't well. *(He hands her a glass, which she surreptitiously cleans on her skirt. He pours her a drink.)*

CORAL:   My Scotch?

(BURGESS *smiles.)*

BURGESS:   One should have asked.

CORAL:   You even took my face powder.

BURGESS:   I know. One is such a coward. Still. You came. I thought you'd chuck. *(He raises his glass in a toast.)*

CORAL:   I nearly did. I seem to have trekked halfway across Moscow. Is there something in the Communist Manifesto against taxis? One never sees any. And that woman on the door downstairs!

BURGESS:   I know. How did you get past her?

CORAL:   I gave her my lipstick.

BURGESS:   I can't think what she'll do with it. I'm always struck by her pronounced resemblance to the late Ernest Bevin. They could be sisters.

CORAL:   Did you enjoy the play?

BURGESS:  What play?

CORAL:  Our play. *Hamlet.*

BURGESS:  Loved it. Loved it. I liked the look of Laertes. He goes rather well into tights.

CORAL:  That's what he thinks.

BURGESS:  He looked as if he'd put a couple of King Edwards down there. That apart, of course, such a pleasure to hear the language so beautifully spoken.

CORAL:  I was told you were asleep.

BURGESS:  No. Though one did have a tiny zizz. After all, one has seen it before. Are there still a couple of music-hall comedians on the wireless called Nat Mills and Bobby?

CORAL:  I don't know them.

BURGESS:  Their catchphrase was, 'Well, why don't you get on with it'? I always feel they would have come in handy in *Hamlet.* Still. The comrades lapped it up. But they do, of course, culture. How do you like Moscow?

CORAL:  Loathe it, darling. I cannot understand what those Three Sisters were on about. It gives the play a very sinister slant.

(*She walks about the flat.*)

BURGESS:  It's hardly luxury's lap, I'm afraid. A pigsty, in fact. I used to live in Jermyn Street. Tragic, you might think, but not really. That was a pigsty, too. By their standards it's quite commodious. Palatial even. One is very lucky.

CORAL:  What is that smell?

BURGESS:  Me probably.

CORAL:  No. Besides that. If it's our lunch, it's burning.

BURGESS:  Oh. Now. It might be. (*He gets up unhurriedly and goes into the kitchenette.*) Yes, it is. It was stew. (*He peers into the pan.*) One could salvage some of it? (*He shows it to* CORAL.)

CORAL:  Hardly.

BURGESS:  Perhaps not. (*He returns to the kitchen with it.*) How-

ever. All is not lost. I managed to scrounge two tomatoes this
morning, and . . . quite a talking point . . . a grapefruit. Shall
we perch? I generally do.

(*He draws* CORAL's *chair to the table and himself sits on
the arm of the easy chair.*)

CORAL:    (*Faintly*) Treats.

(*He puts a tomato on her plate and eats his like an apple.*)

BURGESS:    Garlic?

CORAL:    No, thank you.

BURGESS:    I love it. (*He eats several cloves.*) Yum yum. Now. Tell
me all the gossip. Do you see Harold Nicolson?

CORAL:    I *have* seen him. I don't know him.

BURGESS:    Oh, don't you? Nice man. Nice man. What about Cyril
Connolly?

CORAL:    I haven't run into him either.

BURGESS:    Really? That must be quite difficult. He's everywhere.
You know him, of course?

CORAL:    As a matter of fact, no.

BURGESS:    Oh. One somehow remembers everyone knowing everyone else. Everyone I knew knew everyone else. Auden—do you
know him? Pope Hennessy?

CORAL:    (*Manfully*) The theatre's in a terrible state.

BURGESS:    Is it?

CORAL:    Three plays closed on Shaftesbury Avenue in one week.

BURGESS:    That's tragic. Some ballet on ice is coming here. The
comrades are all agog. I'm rather old-fashioned about ice. I used to
direct at Cambridge, you know. That's how I know your star, Mr
Redgrave. I directed him in *Captain Brassbound's Conversion.* It was
an average production, but notable for a memorable performance by
Arthur Marshall as Lady Cicely Waynflete. Happy days. One thinks
back and wonders, did one miss one's way. What would have
happened had one gone into the theatre? Nothing, I suppose.

CORAL:  Who knows, you might just have been Kenneth Tynan's cup of tea.

BURGESS:  Oh, do you think so? Do you know him?

CORAL:  Slightly.

BURGESS:  He happened after we came away. You're not eating your tomato.

CORAL:  I'm not hungry.

BURGESS:  I am. (*He takes it.*) This garlic!

CORAL:  Do you see many people here?

BURGESS:  Oh yes. Heaps of chums. You don't know what you're missing with this tomato.

CORAL:  There's your other half, I suppose.

BURGESS:  What? Oh yes. He's taken up the balalaika. We play duets.

CORAL:  Maclean?

BURGESS:  No. Oh *no*. Not Maclean. (*He bursts out laughing.*) Taking up the balalaika! Maclean's not my friend. Oh, ducky. Oh no, not Maclean. He's so unfunny, no jokes, no jokes at all. Positively the last person one would have chosen if one had had the choice. And here we are on this terrible tandem together— Debenham and Freebody, Crosse and Blackwell, Auden and Isherwood, Burgess and Maclean. Do you know Auden?

CORAL:  You asked me. No.

BURGESS:  (*Going over to the kitchenette*) Sweet man. Don't look. The seeds get inside my plate. (*He swills his teeth.*) People ask me if I have any regrets. The one regret I have is that before I came away I didn't get kitted out with a good set of National Health gnashers. Admirable as most things are in the Soviet Socialist Republic, the making of dentures is still in its infancy. (*Pause.*) Actually, there's no one in Moscow at all. It's like staying up in Cambridge for the Long Vac. One makes do with whoever's around.

CORAL:  Me.

BURGESS:  No, no. And in any case I asked you here for a reason. Did you bring a tape measure?

CORAL:  I did. (*She produces it.*)

BURGESS:  Good. (BURGESS *puts on his jacket. His suit is well cut but shabby, the knees of the trousers darned and darned again.*) I want you to measure me for some suits. From my tailor. I only have one suit. It's the one I came away in and I've fallen down a lot since then.

CORAL:  But I shan't know where to start. What measurements will he want?

BURGESS:  Measure it all. He'll work it out. He's a nice man. (*He gets her pencil and paper. She draws the figure of a man on the paper.*)

CORAL:  Won't your people here get you a suit?

BURGESS:  What people?

CORAL:  The authorities.

BURGESS:  Oh yes, but have you seen them? Clothes have never been the comrades' strong point. Besides, I don't want to look like everybody else, do I? (*He bends his arm for her to measure.*) I seem to remember doing this.

CORAL:  Your arms can't have altered.

BURGESS:  I never cared tuppence for clothes before . . . Measure me round here . . . I was kitted out in the traditional clothes of my class. Black coat, striped trousers. Pinstripe suit and tweeds for weekends. Shit order, of course. Always in shit order. But charm, I always had charm.

CORAL:  (*Measuring away*) You still have charm. She said through clenched teeth.

BURGESS:  But not here. Not for them. For charm one needs words. I have no words. And, short of my clothes, no class. I am 'The Englishman'. 'Would you like to go to bed with the Englishman'? I say. Not particularly. One got so spoiled during the war. The joys of the black-out. London awash with rude soldiery. (*He says a Russian phrase.*) *Skolko zeem, skolko let.*

CORAL:   What does that mean?

BURGESS:   *Skolko zeem, skolko let?* It means the same as our '*Ou sont les neiges d'antan'?* Nostalgia, you see, knows no frontiers.

CORAL:   Do you speak Russian?

BURGESS:   I manage. Maclean's learned it, naturally, Swot. I haven't. I ought to, simply for the sex. Boys are quite thin on the ground here. I can't speak their language and they can't speak mine, so when one does manage to get one it soon palls. Sex needs language.

(CORAL *is still busy, measuring.*)

CORAL:   At least you've found a friend.

BURGESS:   Tolya? Yes. Except I'm not sure whether I've found him or been allotted him. I know what I've done to be given him. But what has he done to be given me? Am I a reward or a punishment? He plays the balalaika. I play the pianola. It's fun. He's an electrician with the ballet. Of course he may be a policeman. If he is a policeman he's a jolly good actor. Forster lived with a policeman, didn't he? You know him?

(CORAL *shakes her head.*)

Nice man. Getting on now, I suppose.

CORAL:   I feel I'm somewhat of a disappointment in the friends department. I gather Paul Robeson is coming here. Now I know him.

BURGESS:   Do you? He's a big favourite with the comrades. What with being black, and red. I remember when I was posted to the Washington Embassy the Secretary of State, dear old Hector McNeill, had me in his room and gave me a lecture about what I should and shouldn't do when I got there: I mustn't be too openly left-wing, mustn't get involved in the colour question, and above all must avoid homosexual incidents. I said, 'To sum up, Hector, what you're saying is, "Don't make a pass at Paul Robeson" '.

CORAL:   I wouldn't either. Though he did make a pass at me.

BURGESS:   Really? Successfully?

CORAL:   Nobody will believe me when I go home. 'What did you do in Moscow, darling'? 'Nothing much, I measured Guy Burgess's inside leg'.

BURGESS: I shouldn't think one's inside leg alters, do you? It's one of the immutables. 'The knee is such a distance from the main body, whereas the groin, as your honour knows, is upon the very curtain of the place'.

CORAL: Come again.

BURGESS: *Tristram Shandy.* Lovely book. Of course, you wouldn't do that.

CORAL: Do what?

BURGESS: Go round telling everybody. My people here wouldn't like that.

CORAL: (*Looking up from her knees*) No?

BURGESS: No. A hat would be nice. I've written down the name of my hatters. And my bootmakers.

CORAL: It's a trousseau.

BURGESS: Yes. For a shotgun marriage.

CORAL: How do you know he won't say no, your tailor?

BURGESS: Why should he say no? It would be vulgar to say no.

CORAL: Well, I'll see what I can do.

(*She prepares to go.* BURGESS *doesn't make any move.*)

BURGESS: Don't go yet. I don't want you to go yet. You mustn't go yet.

CORAL: Can't we go somewhere? You could show me the sights.

BURGESS: In due course. But we can't go yet. I have to wait for a telephone call. When the telephone call comes I'm permitted to leave.

CORAL: Who from?

BURGESS: Oh . . . you know . . . my people. It's generally around four.

CORAL:    That's another two hours.

BURGESS:    Yes. 'What then is to be done'? as Vladimir Ilyich almost said. I know. I can play you my record.

> (*He puts a record on a gramophone. It is Jack Buchanan singing 'Who stole my heart away'? They listen to this in its entirety.*)

Good, isn't it? It's Jack Buchanan.

CORAL:    Yes.

BURGESS:    Is he still going?

CORAL:    Yes.

BURGESS:    Did you ever come across him?

CORAL:    Yes. I did actually. We nearly got married.

BURGESS:    And?

CORAL:    He jilted me.

BURGESS:    Oh. Small world. Still. It's a good record. (*He puts it on again.*)

CORAL:    And so we sat there in that dreary flat all through that long afternoon waiting for the telephone to ring. From time to time he played his record and I had to listen to my ex-beau. I was puzzled as to how he had managed to get all his books there.

BURGESS:    Someone sent them. A well-wisher. The desk belonged to Stendhal.

CORAL:    Did you have that in London?

BURGESS:    Yes.

CORAL:    Couldn't the same person who sent you your books get you the suits?

BURGESS:    No.

CORAL:    No?

BURGESS:    No.

CORAL:   When I came into the flats I noticed a boy sitting on the stairs playing chess.

BURGESS:   Police. When I first came I used to be shadowed by rather grand policemen. That was when I was a celebrity. Nowadays they just send the trainees. I wish I could lead them a dance. But I can't think of a dance to lead them.

Mind you, they're more conscientious than their English counterparts. All that last week before we left we were tailed—Maclean lived in Sussex. So on the Friday evening we went to Waterloo, dutifully followed by these two men in raincoats. They saw us as far as the barrier and then went home. On the very civilized principle, I suppose, that nothing happens at the weekend. It was the only reason we got away. (*Pause.*) Waterloo the same, is it?

CORAL:   Yes. (*Pause.*) What do you miss most?

BURGESS:   Apart from the Reform Club, the streets of London, and occasionally the English countryside, the only thing I truly miss is gossip. The comrades, though splendid in every other respect, don't gossip in quite the way we do, about quite the same subjects.

CORAL:   Pardon me for saying so, dear, but the comrades seem to me a sad disappointment in every department. There's no gossip, their clothes are terrible, and they can't make false teeth. What else is there?

BURGESS:   (*Gently*) The system. Only, being English, you wouldn't be interested in that. (*Pause.*) My trouble is, I lack what the English call character. By which they mean the power to refrain. Appetite. The English never like that, do they? Unconcealed appetite. For success. Women. Money. Justice. Appetite makes them uncomfortable. What do people say about me in England?

CORAL:   They don't much any more.

(*She gets up and starts tidying up the room. Folding clothes, washing dishes.* BURGESS *watches.*)

I thought of you as a bit like Oscar Wilde.

BURGESS:   No, no. Though he was a performer. And I was a performer. Both vain. But I never pretended. If I wore a mask it was to be exactly what I seemed. And I made no bones about, politics. My analysis of situations, the précis I had to submit at the Foreign Office, were always Marxist. Openly so. Impeccably so. Nobody minded. 'It's only Guy'. 'Dear old Guy'. Quite safe. If you don't wish to conform in one thing, you should conform in all the others. And in all the important things I did conform. 'How can he be a spy? He goes to my tailor'. The average Englishman, you see, is not interested in ideas. You can say what you like about political theory and no one will listen. You could shove a slice of the Communist Manifesto in the Queen's Speech and no one would turn a hair. Least of all, I suspect, HMQ. Am I boring you?

CORAL:   It doesn't matter. (*She investigates the bookshelves. Takes a book out. Puts it back.*)

BURGESS:   I'll think of a hundred and one things to ask you when you've gone. How is Cyril Connolly?

CORAL:   You've asked me that. I don't know.

BURGESS:   You won't have come across Anthony Blunt then?

CORAL:   No. Isn't he quite grand?

BURGESS:   Very grand. That's art. Art is grand. Art and opera. It's the way to get on.

CORAL:   Is he nice?

BURGESS:   Not particularly. Though nice is what you generally have to be, isn't it? 'Is he nice'? So little, England. Little music. Little art. Timid, tasteful, nice. But one loves it. Loves it. You see, I can say I love London. I can say I love England. But I can't say I love my country. I don't know what that means. Do you watch cricket?

CORAL:   No. Anyway, it's changed.

BURGESS:   Cricket?

CORAL:   London.

BURGESS:   Why? I don't want it to change. Why does anybody want to change it? They've no business changing it. The fools. You should stop them changing it. Band together.

CORAL:   Listen, darling. I'm only an actress. Not a bright lady, by your standards. I've never taken much interest in politics. If this is communism I don't like it because it's dull. And the poor dears look so tired. But then Australia is dull and that's not communism. And look at Leeds. Only it occurs to me that we have sat here all afternoon pretending that spying, which is what you did, darling, was just a minor social misdemeanour, no worse—and I'm sure in certain people's minds much better—than being caught in a public lavatory the way gentlemen in my profession constantly are, and that it's just something one shouldn't mention. Out of politeness. So that we won't be embarrassed. That's very English. We will pretend it hasn't happened because we are both civilized people.

Well, I'm not English. And I'm not civilized. I'm Australian. I can't muster much morality, and outside Shakespeare the word treason to me means nothing. Only, you pissed in our soup and we drank it. Very good. Doesn't affect me, darling. And I will order your suit and your hat. And keep it under mine. Mum. Not a word. But for one reason and one reason only: because I'm sorry for you. Now in your book . . . in your *real* book . . . that probably adds my name to the list of all the other fools you've conned. But you're not conning me, darling. Pipe isn't fooling pussy. I know.

(*The telephone rings.*)

BURGESS:   Pity. I was enjoying that. (*He picks up the phone.*) You spoiled the lady's big speech. *Da. Da. Spassibo.* (*He puts the phone down.*) Finished?

CORAL:   I just want to be told why.

BURGESS:   It seemed the right thing to do at the time. And solitude, I suppose.

CORAL:   Solitude?

BURGESS:   If you have a secret you're alone.

CORAL:   But you told people. You told several people.

BURGESS:   No point in having a secret if you make a secret of it. Actually the other thing you might get me is an Etonian tie. This one's on its last legs.

(*They have got up ready to go when* TOLYA, *a young Russian, comes in.*)

Ah, here's Tolya.

*(He kisses him.)*

Tolya. This is Miss Browne. She is an actress. From England.

TOLYA:   *(Pronouncing it very carefully)* How do you do? How are you?

BURGESS:   Very good. If you give him an English cigarette he'll be your friend for life.

*(CORAL does so. TOLYA takes a cigarette but is then fascinated by the packet and takes that also. He examines it carefully then hands it back.)*

CORAL:   No, please. Feel free.

*(CORAL lights his cigarette with her lighter.)*

TOLYA:   Thank you.

*(But now her lighter has caught his eye and he takes that too, flicking it on and off, fascinated.)*

TOLYA:   *Chudyessna.*

BURGESS:   Oh dear. Sorry.

*(Reluctantly TOLYA offers the lighter back.)*

CORAL:   *(Resigned)* No, please.

BURGESS:   *(Taking the lighter and handing it back to CORAL)* No, you mustn't. He'll take anything. He's a real Queen Mary. But you . . . wouldn't be able to order him a suit, would you? Off the peg. He'd look so nice.

CORAL:   *(Desperately)* Anything. Anything.

TOLYA:   *(In Russian)* Ya hotyel bwi eegrat dlya nyeyo.

BURGESS:   *Da? Samnoy?*

TOLYA:   *Konyeshna.*

BURGESS:   Tolya wants us to play you a tune. Let him. He'd be so pleased. Just five minutes.

*(They embark on the duet 'Take a pair of sparkling eyes' from Gilbert and Sullivan's The Gondoliers.)*

BURGESS:   (*Shouts above the music.*) What do you think? Reward or punishment?

(*The music continues as the lights fade, hiding the room.*)

CORAL:   When we left the flat he took me to a church not far from where he lived. I've since been told that it was kept open just to indicate that there still were such places. The singing was very good. Apparently it was where the opera singers went to warm up for the evening's performance.

As a rule I don't have much time for men's tears. It's like blowing smoke rings, crying is a facility some men have. And it wasn't as if there was anything particularly English about the service. It wasn't like church or school, and yet when I looked at him the tears were rolling down his cheeks. He left me outside my hotel.

(CORAL *goes stage right, leaving* BURGESS *in the spot, stage left.*)

BURGESS:   Something else you could do for me when you get back. Ring the old mum. Tell her I'm all right. Looking after myself. She's been here once. Loved it. Too frail now. I would come back to see her but apparently it's not on. Still got to stand in the corner, I suppose.
    'Let him never come back to us.
    There would be doubt, hesitation and pain.
    Forced praise on our part, the glimmer of twilight,
    Never glad confident morning again'.
Good old Browning. Goodbye. *Das vidanya.*

(*The light fades on* BURGESS *as* CORAL *comes on, right, in a different coat and hat.*
    *A* TAILOR *enters, left, wearing a tape measure and carrying a swatch of samples.*)

CORAL:   I'd like to order some suits.

TAILOR:   Certainly madam.

CORAL:   You've made suits for the gentleman before, but he now lives abroad.

TAILOR:   I see.

(CORAL *hands him her bit of paper.*)

CORAL:    I took his measurements. I'm not sure they're the right ones.

(*The* TAILOR *looks at the paper.*)

TAILOR:    Oh yes. These are more than adequate. Could one know the gentleman's name?

CORAL:    Yes. Mr Burgess.

TAILOR:    We have two Mr Burgesses. I take this to be Mr Burgess G. How is Mr Burgess? Fatter, I see. One of our more colourful customers. Too little colour in our drab lives these days. Knowing Mr Guy he'll want a pinstripe. But a durable fabric. His suits were meant to take a good deal of punishment. I hope they have stood him in good stead.

CORAL:    Yes. They have indeed.

TAILOR:    I'm glad to hear it. Always getting into scrapes, Mr Guy. And your name is . . . ?

CORAL:    Browne.

TAILOR:    There is no need for discretion here, madam.

CORAL:    Truly.

TAILOR:    My apologies. (*He looks at her in recognition.*) Of course. And this is the address. I see. We put a little of ourselves into our suits. That is our loyalty.

CORAL:    And mum's the word.

TAILOR:    Oh, madam. Mum is always the word here. Moscow or Maidenhead, mum is always the word.

(*The* TAILOR *exits left leaving* CORAL *in the spot right.*)

CORAL:    And so it was with all the shops I went into, scarcely an eyebrow raised. When the parcels arrived he wrote to me, the letter dated 11 April 1958, Easter Sunday, to which he adds, 'a very suitable day to be writing to you, since I also was born on it, to the later horror of the Establishment of the country concerned'.

(BURGESS, *left, now takes over the letter.*)

BURGESS:    I really find it hard to know how to thank you properly.

Everything *fits*. No need for any alterations at all. Thank you. Thank you. In spite of your suggestion—invitation, to visit your friend Paul Robeson, I find myself too shy to call on him. Not so much shy as frightened. The *agonies* I remember on first meeting with people I really admire, E. M. Forster (and Picasso and Winston Churchill). H. G. Wells was quite different, but one could get drunk with him and listen to stories of his sex life. Fascinating. How frightened one would be of Charlie Chaplin.

One more thing. What I really need, the only thing more, is pyjamas. Russian ones can't be slept in, are not in fact made for the purpose. What I would like if you can find it is four pairs of white or off-white pyjamas . . .

(A SHOP ASSISTANT *brings on a chair, right.*)

ASSISTANT:    If you could take a seat, madam, I'll just check.

CORAL:    '. . . *Four* pairs. Quite plain and only those two colours. Then at last my outfit will be complete and I shall look like a real agent again'. (*She looks twice.*) 'Then I shall look like a real gent again'.

(The SHOP ASSISTANT *returns.*)

ASSISTANT:    I'm afraid, madam, that the gentleman in question no longer has an account with us. His account was closed.

CORAL:    I know. He wishes to open it again.

ASSISTANT:    I'm afraid that's not possible.

CORAL:    Why?

ASSISTANT:    Well . . . we supply pyjamas to the Royal Family.

CORAL:    So?

ASSISTANT:    The gentleman is a traitor, madam.

CORAL:    So? Must traitors sleep in the buff?

ASSISTANT:    I'm sorry. We have to draw the line somewhere.

CORAL:    So why here? Say someone commits adultery in your precious nightwear. I imagine it has occurred. What happens when he comes in to order his next pair of jim-jams. Is it sorry, no can do?

ASSISTANT:   I'm very sorry.

CORAL:   (*Her Australian accent gets now more pronounced as she gets crosser.*) You keep saying you're sorry, dear. You were quite happy to satisfy this client when he was one of the most notorious buggers in London and a drunkard into the bargain. Only then he was in the Foreign Office. 'Red piping on the sleeve, Mr Burgess—but of course'. 'A discreet monogram on the pocket, Mr Burgess'? Certainly. And perhaps if you'd be gracious enough to lower your trousers, Mr Burgess, we could be privileged enough to thrust our tongue between the cheeks of your arse. But not any more. Oh no. Because the gentleman in question has shown himself to have some principles, principles which aren't yours and, as a matter of interest, aren't mine. But that's it, as far as you're concerned. No more jamas for him. I tell you, it's pricks like you that make me understand why he went. Thank Christ I'm not English.

ASSISTANT:   As a matter of fact, madam, our firm isn't English either.

CORAL:   Oh? What is it?

ASSISTANT:   Hungarian. (*He exits right.*)

CORAL:   Oh, I said, and thinking of the tanks going into Budapest a year or two before, wished I hadn't made such a fuss. So I went down the street to Simpsons and got him some pyjamas there. Guy wrote to thank me and sent me a cheque for £6 to treat myself to supper at the Caprice. Which one could, of course, in those days. In those days. Anyway, that was the last I heard of him. He never did come back, of course, dying in 1963. Heart attack.

This comedy I was in at the Cambridge, *Affairs of State*—I played the wife of an elderly statesman. 'Your friends were great men in their time', I had to say, 'only those who've managed to stay alive can now hardly manage to stay awake'. And that of course, would have been the solution for Burgess, to live on to a great age. Had he been living now he would have been welcomed back with open arms, just as Mosley was a few years back. He could have written his memoirs, gone on all the chat shows, done *Desert Island Discs* . . . played his Jack Buchanan record again. In England, you see, age wipes the slate clean. (*She gets up.*) If you live to be ninety in England and can still eat a boiled egg they think you deserve the Nobel Prize.

*(Now smartly suited, wearing an overcoat and Homburg hat and carrying an umbrella* BURGESS *stands in the spot stage left, the picture of an upper-class Englishman. Accompanied as if on the pianola he starts to sing 'For he is an Englishman' from Gilbert and Sullivan's* HMS Pinafore.)*

BURGESS:    For he might have been a Roosian,
A French or Turk or Proosian,
Or perhaps I-tal-ian.
For in spite of all temptations
To belong to other nations,
He remains an Englishman,
He remains an Englishman.

*(As* BURGESS *sings he is drowned out by the full chorus and orchestra in a rousing climax, but before the music stops the light has faded on* BURGESS *and the screen drops in, bright and blank and* CORAL *stands in front of it as though after a film screening.)*

CORAL:    At supper one night, after a showing of the film of this story in 1983, I met Lord Harlech, who as David Ormsby-Gore had been Minister of State at the Foreign Office at the time Burgess was wanting to come back and see his mother. The Foreign Office and the security services were in a blue funk apparently. All the threats of prosecution that were conveyed to Burgess were pure bluff. Harlech said there was nothing it would have been safe to charge him with. Egg on too many faces, I suppose.

'And what about the others'? I said. 'What others'? he said. I said I'd heard there were others. Still. But he just smiled.

# A Question of Attribution

AN INQUIRY IN WHICH
THE CIRCUMSTANCES ARE IMAGINARY
BUT THE PICTURES ARE REAL

FIGURE 1

FIGURE 2

FIGURE 3

FIGURE 4

# A Question of Attribution

A NOTE ON THE PAINTINGS

A *Question of Attribution* is concerned with two paintings, Titian's *Allegory of Prudence* in the National Gallery and *Triple Portrait*, formerly attributed to Titian, which is in the collection of HM The Queen. The play owes a great deal to two articles in which these paintings are discussed, 'Titian's *Allegory of Prudence*' by Erwin Panofsky (in *Meaning in the Visual Arts*, Peregrine, 1974) and 'Five Portraits' by St John Gore (*Burlington Magazine*, vol. 100, 1958).

For understandable reasons we were not permitted to reproduce the actual *Triple Portrait* for the stage production. Fortunately there was a copy of the original at Hardwick Hall, though this copy only included the original two figures. The 'third man', who was revealed when the royal picture was cleaned, was not in the Hardwick Hall version, which must therefore have been copied after he had been painted out. For the stage production we reproduced the Hardwick Hall version, courtesy of the National Trust, and the 'third man' was added to the picture by the graphics department at the National Theatre. Though its shortcomings make the comparison with Titian's son, Orazio Vecelli, less than convincing, should anyone be interested enough to compare the two from the actual paintings they would, I think, find that the identification is certainly arguable.

At the moment, however, such a comparison would be difficult to make as the *Triple Portrait* cannot be seen. It used to hang at Hampton Court but since the fire there in 1986 it has not been on public view. Indeed, I have never seen it myself, knowing it only from the photographs which illustrate Mr St John Gore's article. There is a certain appropriateness about this, though, as one of the criticisms made of Anthony Blunt as an art historian was that he preferred to work from photographs rather than the real thing.

CHARACTERS

BLUNT

CHUBB

PHILLIPS

HMQ

COLIN

RESTORER

# A Question of Attribution

ANTHONY BLUNT'S *room at the Courtauld Institute where he is the Director. The time is the late 1960s. There is a large eighteenth-century double door and a fine ormolu mounted table serving as a desk but in all other respects the room is a functioning office, the bookshelves crowded with reference books and with piles of octavo volumes on the floor. Above the desk and upstage of it is a projection screen with a slide projector on a nearby side-table.*

BLUNT *stands left of the screen and the* RESTORER, *a humbler figure in a dustcoat, to the right. Their positions resemble those of saints or patrons on either side of an altarpiece and some effort should be made in the production to create stage pictures which echo in this way the composition and lighting of old masters.*

BLUNT: Next.

(*On the screen a slide of the* Triple Portrait *before cleaning* [Figure 1].)

RESTORER: More of the same, I'm afraid. It's an ex-Titian. Now thought to be by several hands.

BLUNT: Called?

(*The* RESTORER *consults a catalogue or printed sheet.*)

RESTORER: *Titian and a Venetian Senator.*

BLUNT: And this is Titian on the left. He's not by Titian, certainly.

RESTORER: No. He's a copy of the Berlin self-portrait.

BLUNT: I don't know about the other gentleman.

41

RESTORER:   He's been identified as the Chancellor of Venice, Andrea Franceschi.

(*Pause.*)

BLUNT:   I should warn you. I don't have an eye. Kenneth Clark was saying the other day (I don't *think* the remark was directed at me) that people who look at old masters fall into three groups: those who see what it is without being told; those who see it when you tell them; and those who can't see it whatever you do. I just about make the second category. It means I can't date pictures. Made a terrible hash of the early Poussins. Couldn't tell which came first. For an art historian it's rather humiliating. Like being a wine taster and having no sense of smell. (*Pause.*) People find me cold. I don't gush, I suppose.

RESTORER:   Not much to gush about, this lot. Mind you, wait till you see Holyrood.

BLUNT:   I'm not saying painting doesn't affect me. Ravished, sometimes. Well, what do we do? Give it a scrub?

RESTORER:   Couldn't do any harm.

BLUNT:   On. On.

(*A slide of a painting of St Lawrence being roasted over a grid comes up on the screen.*)

What frightful thing is happening here?

RESTORER:   *The Martyrdom of St Lawrence.*

(BLUNT *groans.*)

BLUNT:   Art!

(BLUNT *steps from the office set to a podium or lectern, stage left, and we should have a sense that he is in the middle of a lecture. The lecture is illustrated by slides projected on the screen; these slides include Giovanni Bellini's* Agony in the Garden, *an* Annunciation *and other appropriate images, details and martyrdoms.*)

BLUNT:   Were we not inured to its imagery, however, it would seem a curious world, this world of Renaissance art; a place of incongruous punishments, where heads come on plates and skulls sport cleavers, and an angel—tremulous as a butterfly—waits patiently for the attention of a young girl who is pretending to read.

Doomed to various slow and ingenious extinctions the saints brandish the emblems of their suffering—the cross, the gridiron and the wheel—and submit to their fate readily and without fuss, howling agonies gone through without a murmur, the only palliative a vision of God and the assurance of Heaven. Remote though all this is from our sensibility, there is a sense in which one might feel that it is all very British. For flayed, dismembered, spitted, roasted, these martyrs seldom lose a drop of their *sang-froid,* so cool about their bizarre torments, the real emblems of their martyrdom a silk dressing-gown and a long cigarette-holder; all of them doing their far, far better thing in a dignified silence. About suffering they were always wrong, the old masters. (*Slide.*)

In Bellini's *Agony in the Garden,* for instance, the apostles—oblivious to all considerations but those of perspective—are fast asleep on ground as brown and bare as an end-of-the-season goal-mouth, this sleep signifying indifference. Above them on a rocky promontory of convenient geology, Jesus kneels in prayer, an exercise that still goes on in some places, though with less agony and less certainty of address, this praying of less interest to the budding art historian or to the social historian or even to someone who has just wandered into the gallery out of the rain (and it is salutary to remind ourselves, here at the Courtauld Institute, that that is what art is for most people) . . . this praying, as I say, of less interest to them than the reaper on the edge of a field in a Breughel, say, who has his hand up a woman's dress, another exercise that still goes on in most places, though with no agony but the same certainty of address. Here is threshing, which we now do mechanically. Here is sex, which we do mechanically also. And here is crucifixion, which we do not do, or do differently. Or do indifferently. It is a world in which time means nothing, the present overlaps the future, and did the saint but turn his head he would see his own martyrdom through the window.

(*On the other side of the stage, right, we see the double doors open to reveal a man in trilby and raincoat, carrying a briefcase. This is* CHUBB.)

Judas takes the pieces of silver in the Temple at the same moment as in the next field he hangs himself. Christ begs God in the garden to free him from a fate that is already happening higher up the hill.

(As *the lectern or podium disappears* BLUNT *steps back into the office where* CHUBB *is waiting.* CHUBB *is seemingly vague, seemingly amiable. Socially he is not in the same class as* BLUNT, *who is sophisticated and metropolitan;* CHUBB, *while not naïve, is definitely suburban. The slides on the screen have changed to photographs of various young men, taken singly or enlarged from group photographs of colleges and teams; all date from the thirties and are in black and white. Following each denial by* BLUNT *a new photograph comes up on the screen.*)

BLUNT:  No. No. No. (BLUNT *seems uncertain.*)

CHUBB:  Sure?

BLUNT:  It's the neck. The *neck* could be Piero della Francesca.

CHUBB:  Who's he?

BLUNT:  Well, he was many things, but he wasn't a member of the Communist Party. And in answer to your earlier question, the larger question, I would only say . . . again . . . it seemed the right thing to do at the time.

CHUBB:  One more?

BLUNT:  Do I have a choice?

(CHUBB *switches off the screen.*)

CHUBB:  You're probably tired.

BLUNT:  Not particularly.

CHUBB:  All these functions.

BLUNT:  I don't go to what you call 'functions'.

CHUBB:  If you're in charge of the Queen's pictures you must often have to be in attendance.

BLUNT:  Yes. On the pictures.

CHUBB:  I'm disappointed. Don't you see the Queen?

BLUNT:  The Crown is a large organization. To ask me if I see the Queen is like asking a shopgirl if she sees Fortnum or Mason.

CHUBB: My wife saw her the other day. When she was visiting Surrey.

BLUNT: Your wife?

CHUBB: The Queen. She was up at six o'clock and secured an excellent vantage point outside Bentall's. Her Majesty was heard to say 'What a splendid shopping centre'. I wonder what she's really like.

BLUNT: Look her up. You must have a file on her.

CHUBB: Yes, we probably do. I meant, to chat to. Hob-nob with. As a person. You can't, of course, say. I appreciate that.

BLUNT: Why can't I say?

CHUBB: Royal servants can't, can they? Keeping mum is part of the job. It's like the Official Secrets Act. (*Pause.*) I'm sorry. That was unkind. More snaps?

(BLUNT *says nothing.*)

Some people do this for pleasure, you know. Holidays. Trips abroad. 'This is a delightful couple we ran into on the boat; he's in the Foreign Office and he's a lorry driver'. You must get asked round to watch people's slides.

BLUNT: Never.

CHUBB: You don't live in Purley.

BLUNT: No.

(CHUBB *switches on the screen with another photograph.*)

How many more times. There is no one else that I know.

CHUBB: This morning I got up, cup of tea, read the *Telegraph*, the usual routine. Nothing on the agenda for today, I thought, why not toddle up to town and wander round the British Museum, sure to come across something of interest. Just turning into Great Russell Street when I remember there is something on the agenda. Your good self! What's more, I'm due at the Courtauld Institute in five minutes. So I about turn and head for Portman Square.

(*Pause.*)

BLUNT: And? I was under the impression this narrative was leading somewhere.

CHUBB: The point is, we sometimes know things we don't know. A bit of me, you see, must have known that I was coming here. (*He switches the screen off.*) Have you ever caught Her Majesty in an unguarded moment?

BLUNT: I thought it was my unguarded moments you were interested in.

CHUBB: It's just a titbit for my wife.

BLUNT: My function here is not to provide your wife with fodder for the hairdresser's.

CHUBB: She thinks my job is so dull.

BLUNT: And mine?

CHUBB: I'm sure you have colleagues who'd be delighted to be in your shoes.

BLUNT: Really? Having to see you all the time?

CHUBB: Oh. I was under the impression you enjoyed these little get-togethers. I always do.

BLUNT: You nearly forgot.

CHUBB: I forgot it was *today*. I thought you looked forward to these little chats. I thought it helped you relax. 'All the time'. It's only once a month. I now feel I'm a burden. (*Pause.*) We could always scrap them. It's true we don't seem to be getting anywhere.

BLUNT: I wouldn't want that.

CHUBB: You've only to say the word. I don't know, I must have got hold of the wrong end of the stick. I thought this was the way you wanted it.

BLUNT: It is. It is.

CHUBB: The alternative isn't ruled out. If you feel that . . .

BLUNT: I don't feel that at all. I . . . I had a late night.

CHUBB: You *were* at the Palace!

BLUNT: Initially, yes.

CHUBB:    I knew you were. My wife saw your name in the paper. Well, I'm not surprised you're tired. You must always be on tenterhooks, frightened to put a foot wrong, having to watch every word. You must find it a terrible strain.

BLUNT:    Talking to you?

CHUBB:    No. Talking to Her Majesty. What is she really like?

BLUNT:    Should we look at some more photographs?

CHUBB:    In a moment. I'm upset that you find our talks wearisome.

BLUNT:    I don't. I don't. It was an unforgivable remark. And not the case. On the whole I find them  .  .  .  stimulating.

CHUBB:    Do you? Now truthfully.

BLUNT:    They keep me on my toes.

CHUBB:    I'm glad. Are you liked, by the way?

BLUNT:    By whom?

CHUBB:    I don't know. It occurs to me that you work rather hard at being a cold fish.

BLUNT:    My pupils like me. My colleagues  .  .  .  I don't know. I have a life, you see. Two lives. Some of my colleagues scarcely have one.

CHUBB:    They don't know about your other life.

BLUNT:    In the Household.

CHUBB:    I see. In that case, three lives. But who's counting. (*He laughs. Suddenly switches on the screen with a new photograph.*) You don't know this boy? Not a boy now, of course. Might have a beard.

BLUNT:    Should I? Who is he?

CHUBB:    Nobody.

(*The next photograph is of a guardsman in uniform.*)

BLUNT:    No.

(*The same guardsman now naked.*)

CHUBB:    Goodness gracious. How did that get here? Dear me. Just think if one of your students knocked at the door. Two gentlemen looking at a picture of a naked guardsman. What would they think?

BLUNT:    They might think it was Art, or they might think it was two gentlemen looking at a picture of a naked guardsman. They would be profoundly unstartled by either.

(CHUBB *switches off the screen.*)

CHUBB:    Do you ever go to the National Gallery?

BLUNT:    One has to from time to time. Though I avoid opening hours. The public make it so intolerable.

CHUBB:    I went in the other day.

BLUNT:    Really?

CHUBB:    First time in yonks.

BLUNT:    Good.

CHUBB:    No, not good. Not good at all, better off sticking to museums. Museums I know where I am. An art gallery, I always come out feeling restless and dissatisfied. Troubled.

BLUNT:    Oh dear.

CHUBB:    In a museum I'm informed, instructed. But with art . . . I don't know. Is it that I don't get anything out of the pictures? Or the pictures don't get anything out of me? What am I supposed to think? What am I supposed to feel?

BLUNT:    What do you feel?

CHUBB:    Baffled. And also knackered. I ended up on a banquette looking at the painting that happened to be opposite and I thought, well, at least I can try to take this one in. But no. Mind you, I hate shopping. I suppose for you an art gallery is home from home.

BLUNT:    Some more than others. Home is hardly the word for the Hayward.

CHUBB:    But you'll know, for instance, what order they all come in, the paintings?

BLUNT:    Well . . . one does . . . quite early on . . . acquire a sense of the sequence, the chronology of art. Shouldn't we be getting on?

CHUBB:   You see, I don't have that. I've no map. And yet I know there's a whole world there.

BLUNT:   Yes.

CHUBB:   I'm determined to crack it. I'm like that. A year ago I couldn't have changed a fuse. Started going down to the library, the odd evening class: I've just rewired the whole house. What I thought I'd do with this was start at the beginning before artists had really got the hang of it . . . perspective, for instance, a person and a house the same size (I can't understand how they couldn't just see). And then I'm planning to follow it through until they start painting what is actually—you know—*there*. How does that strike you as an approach? It's not too sophisticated?

BLUNT:   No. One couldn't honestly say that. It incorporates one or two misconceptions, which it would not at this stage be very useful to go into. Mustn't run before we can walk.

CHUBB:   Tell me; I don't want to get off on the wrong foot.

BLUNT:   Shouldn't we be looking at more photographs?

CHUBB:   In a minute. The chronological approach is a mistake?

BLUNT:   Not in itself. But art has no goal. It evolves but it does not necessarily progress. Just as the history of politics isn't simply a progress towards parliamentary democracy, so the history of painting isn't simply a progress towards photographic realism. Different periods have different styles, different ways of seeing the world. And what about the Impressionists or Matisse or Picasso?

CHUBB:   Oh, I think they could do it properly if they wanted to. They just got bored.

(BLUNT *is exasperated.*)

That's the way art galleries are arranged. Crude beginnings, growing accomplishment, mastery of all the techniques . . . then to hell with the rules, let's kick it around a bit.

BLUNT:   But why should a plausible illusion of nature be the standard? Do we say Giotto isn't a patch on Michelangelo because his figures are less lifelike?

CHUBB:   Michelangelo? I don't think they are all that lifelike, frankly. The women aren't. They're just like men with tits, and the tits look as if they've been put on with an ice-cream scoop. Has nobody pointed that out?

BLUNT:   Not in quite those terms.

CHUBB:   Are you sure your students like you?

BLUNT:   Discussion is seldom at this level.

CHUBB:   You're finding me wearisome again.

BLUNT:   These painters—Giotto, Piero—they aren't so many failed Raphaels, Leonardos without the know-how. Try to look at them as contemporaries did, judge them on their own terms—not as prefiguring some (to them) unknown future. They didn't know Raphael was going to do it better.

CHUBB:   To be quite honest I haven't got to Raphael. But where have I heard that argument before?

BLUNT:   If you were planning on going to the British Museum, how was it you remembered to bring the photographs?

CHUBB:   I know. It's exactly the same argument you were using to explain what you did in the thirties: it seemed the right thing to do at the time. Giotto didn't have a grasp on perspective and neither did you. The difference being, of course, that art has no consequences.

BLUNT:   How did you remember the photographs?

CHUBB:   I didn't. I nipped up to the office for them. Good try, though. (*He switches on the screen and the photographs start again.*)

BLUNT:   No.

(*Photo.*)

No.

(Titian and a Venetian Senator *now comes up on the screen as we saw it in the opening scene with two figures* [Figure 1].)

RESTORER:   This was before cleaning. (*He punches up a slide of the picture after cleaning, now with a third figure* [Figure 2].) This is after cleaning.

BLUNT:  I thought there must be something there. With just the two of them, it didn't make sense as a composition.

RESTORER:  Quite. Though it doesn't make a lot of sense as a composition now.

BLUNT:  No?

RESTORER:  Look at Titian. The scale is all wrong. He looks as if he belongs in a different picture.

BLUNT:  He does, of course. It's a copy.

RESTORER:  Yes.

BLUNT:  From the Berlin self-portrait.

RESTORER:  Yes.

BLUNT:  But at least we know who he is. And who the Chancellor is. But who is the new man? An X-ray, do you think?

RESTORER:  Can't do any harm.

BLUNT:  Wish it were a better picture. Got the velvet rather well.

(*The restorer disappears as a photograph of more young men comes up on the screen.*)

CHUBB:  And who is the other figure?

BLUNT:  I don't know.

CHUBB:  You've identified him before in a different context.

BLUNT:  So why are you asking me again?

CHUBB:  It's the context we're interested in.

(*Photograph.*)

Who's this?

BLUNT:  His name was Baker. He was at Oxford. Balliol, possibly.

CHUBB:  Handsome.

BLUNT:  Is he?

CHUBB:  Isn't he?

BLUNT:    Dead, anyway.

CHUBB:    Naturally. When was that?

BLUNT:    The death?

CHUBB:    The photograph.

BLUNT:    August Bank Holiday, 1935. Margate.

CHUBB:    Vanished world. Hooligans on scooters nowadays.

(*Photograph.*)

Who are these gentlemen?

BLUNT:    Chums of Burgess. Cameron Highlanders, I think. Kilted jobs anyway.

CHUBB:    Two in a row. Progress.

BLUNT:    Not really. I don't suppose they had access to any information above latrine roster level.

CHUBB:    They probably had other qualities.

BLUNT:    I once had a photograph of Burgess with his head under one of their kilts.

(*Photograph.*)

CHUBB:    This one?

(*Pause.*)

BLUNT:    Yes.

CHUBB:    Odd, isn't it, that it's the irrelevant details that you can recall. An August Bank Holiday in Margate. Not Worthing. Not the Seaforth Highlanders but the Camerons. (CHUBB *drops several slides on the floor. He picks them up.*) Facts, faces, you might be expected to remember you forget.

BLUNT:    That's the way with memory. The canvas is vague. The details stand out.

CHUBB:    It could get tiresome.

(*Photograph.*)

BLUNT:    No.

(*Photograph.*)

No.

(A *slide of Titian's* Allegory of Prudence *has come up on the screen, in colour* [Figure 3].)

N—Oh yes.

CHUBB:    Sorry. Must have picked up one of yours.

BLUNT:    No. Leave it. At least I can tell you their names. But perhaps you know it. It's in the National Gallery. How far have you got on your safari through the nation's masterpieces? Have you reached Titian?

CHUBB:    Don't tell me. Venetian. Sixteenth century. A contemporary of Tintoretto and Veronese. In some sense the founder of modern painting.

BLUNT:    In what sense?

CHUBB:    Well, in the sense that he painted character.

BLUNT:    Mmm, though it's not the slightest use knowing that unless you recognize one of his pictures when you see one.

CHUBB:    Is this typical?

BLUNT:    Actually, no.

CHUBB:    Ah.

BLUNT:    Though it is Titian at the top of his form. Done towards the end of his life . . .

CHUBB:    Didn't he live until he was ninety-nine?

BLUNT:    That has been disputed. What cannot be disputed is the style, shining with all the autumnal magnificence of his *ultima maniera*.

CHUBB:    Too plush for me, Titian. All fur and fabric. Don't like the look of that dog.

BLUNT:    That's because that dog is a wolf. (*He points to a creature on the right.*) That dog is a dog.

CHUBB:    Still wouldn't want to be the postman. Who are they all?

BLUNT: The old man on the left is Titian himself.

CHUBB: He *looks* ninety-nine.

BLUNT: . . . The middle-aged man in the centre is Titian's son, and the young man on the right is probably his adopted grandson.

CHUBB: I don't care for it, quite honestly.

BLUNT: Oh.

CHUBB: Something of the three wise monkeys about it.

BLUNT: That's not an altogether foolish remark.

CHUBB: Good for Chubb. Why?

BLUNT: Because it's an emblematic painting, a puzzle picture. A visual paraphrase of the *Three Ages of Man*, obviously, but something else besides. The clue is the animals.

CHUBB: Was he fond of animals?

BLUNT: Titian? I've no idea. Shouldn't think so for a moment. People weren't.

CHUBB: Rembrandt was. Rembrandt liked dogs.

BLUNT: Rembrandt's dogs, Titian's age. I can see you've been down at the Purley Public Library again. Except that Rembrandt's dogs are different. Rembrandt's dogs tend to be just dogs. This is hardly a dog at all.

CHUBB: You mean it's a symbol of fidelity?

BLUNT: It can be.

CHUBB: Hence Fido. And the wolf is a symbol of gluttony.

BLUNT: One hopes the security of the nation is not being neglected in favour of your studies in iconography.

CHUBB: One picks it up, you know.

BLUNT: (*Sharply*) Well, if you do 'pick it up', pick it up properly. Yes, a dog is a symbol of fidelity and a wolf of gluttony, but occurring together as they do here, in conjunction with the lion, they are disparate parts of a three-headed beast which from classical times onwards has been a symbol of prudence. Hence the title of the picture: the *Allegory of Prudence*.

CHUBB:   And I thought I was getting the hang of it.

BLUNT:   There isn't a 'hang of it'. There isn't a kit. A wolf can mean gluttony, a dog fidelity, and treachery a cat. But not always. Not automatically. Take the owl. It can be a bird of wisdom, but since it is a bird of the night it can represent the opposite, ignorance and wilful blindness. Hardest of all to accept, it can be just an owl. Of course, one shouldn't blame you. You're just carrying over the techniques of facile   identification   favoured   in   your   profession,   into mine . . . where it isn't quite like that. Appearances deceive. Art is seldom quite what it seems.

CHUBB:   Back to the drawing-board. Perhaps we should do some more.

BLUNT:   Art?

CHUBB:   Facile identification.

   (*Photograph.*)

BLUNT:   No.

   (*Photograph.*)

No. Actually, that face does ring a bell.

CHUBB:   Yes? (*He goes back to the last photograph.*)

BLUNT:   I've seen it.

CHUBB:   Who is he?

BLUNT:   I told you. Titian's son.

CHUBB:   I thought for one delirious moment we were about to make progress.

BLUNT:   Where is it? Come along, come along. This is how you learn.

   (CHUBB *goes back through the photographs until he reaches the Titian again.* BLUNT *stands looking up at the central figure of Titian's son.*)

I have seen him. Where?

(A *knock at the door.* PHILLIPS, *a student, stands silhou-etted in the doorway.*)

PHILLIPS:   It's Phillips, sir.

BLUNT:   I shan't keep you a moment. I have to teach now. Since Mr Phillips is paying for his time I think he has priority. Perhaps you might wait outside, Phillips, we haven't quite finished.

CHUBB:   We haven't even started.

(PHILLIPS *exits.* CHUBB *gathers up the photographs and puts them in his briefcase.*)

I'm not good at cracking the whip. I enjoy our talks.

BLUNT:   (*Consulting a reference book*) So you keep saying.

CHUBB:   Eyebrows are beginning to be raised. The phrase 'stringing you along' has been mentioned. The feeling is, you see, that you may just be the baby thrown out of the sleigh to slow down the wolves.

BLUNT:   And who are these wolves?

CHUBB:   They're like this one (*in the Titian*). They look back. They're the ones with hindsight. You've told us some names. You've not told us the names behind the names.

BLUNT:   Can I ask you something? Who else knows?

CHUBB:   Do you mean, down the road? Somebody had to be told. You were promised immunity, not anonymity. What do you think of the Wallace Collection? Should I go there?

BLUNT:   Their Poussin apart, it's a bit chocolate box.

CHUBB:   They have the *Laughing Cavalier*.

BLUNT:   Exactly. Come in, Phillips.

(CHUBB *leaves as* PHILLIPS *comes in.*)

PHILLIPS:   I've seen him once or twice. He comes into the library.

BLUNT:   Yes. He's a mature student.

PHILLIPS:   I'd say he was a policeman.

BLUNT:   Do you have a suit?

PHILLIPS:   Suit?

BLUNT:   Jacket, trousers, preferably matching. Even, by some sartorial miracle, a waistcoat.

PHILLIPS:   I do, as a matter of fact.

BLUNT:   And is it handy, or is it in Thornton Heath.

PHILLIPS:   I think I can put my hands on it without too much trouble.

BLUNT:   Well, go away and put your hands on it and your legs into it and telephone me here at two o'clock.

PHILLIPS:   Why, what's happening?

BLUNT:   Nothing. A little extra-mural work. Off you go.

(PHILLIPS *goes as the lights fade.* BLUNT *turns to gaze at the* Allegory of Prudence *then switches off the projector as the scene changes.*)


BLUNT'S *room recedes, a red carpet runs the breadth of the stage, gilt console tables appear and an elaborate banquette is set against the wall covered in (not over-exciting) paintings. We are in a corridor of Buckingham Palace and prominent among the paintings hanging on the wall is the* Triple Portrait [Figure 2].

COLIN, *a young footman in an apron, comes on carrying a picture. He puts the picture down as* PHILLIPS, *now in a suit, follows him carrying a step-ladder and looking wonderingly at the pictures and the furniture.*

COLIN:   Jumble. Bric-à-brac.

PHILLIPS:   This is a Raphael.

COLIN:   The regal equivalent of the fish-slice or the chromium cake-stand. A downstairs attic, this corridor. (*Pause.*) And it's not Raphael. It's school of.

PHILLIPS:   How would you know?

COLIN:    Because I dust it.

(PHILLIPS *keeps looking up and down the corridor.*)

Nobody's coming. Sir is out practising with his horse and cart, and Madam is opening a swimming-bath. Though in the unlikely event anyone does come by, disappear. They are happier thinking the place runs itself.

(PHILLIPS *is looking at an ornate clock.*)

Like that, do you?

PHILLIPS:    Liking doesn't necessarily come into it.

COLIN:    It's ormolu. I've always had a soft spot for ormolu. Childhood, I suppose. Ormolu's fairly thin on the ground in Bethnal Green.

(PHILLIPS *is now looking at a painting.*)

PHILLIPS:    Some of these are in terrible condition.

COLIN:    I can't think why. They get a wipe over with a damp cloth quite regularly.

PHILLIPS:    How did you come to work here?

COLIN:    It was either this or the police force. I had the qualifications. Presentable. Good-looking in a standard sort of way. I might even be thought to be public school until I opened my mouth. But of course you don't open your mouth. That's one of the conditions of employment. So are you top boy?

(BLUNT *has come on, unseen by* PHILLIPS.)

PHILLIPS:    What?

COLIN:    Earned yourself a trip to the Palace, you must have something.

BLUNT:    He does. A suit. Fool of a policeman on the gate. Insisted on going through my briefcase. He said, 'Do you have anything explosive'? I said, 'Yes, I certainly do. An article for the *Burlington Magazine* on Sebastiano del Piombo that is going to blow the place sky-high'. Not amused. I've been walking through that gate for ten years.
How are you today, Colin?

COLIN:    Perfectly all right, thank you.

(BLUNT *looks at the* Triple Portrait.)

BLUNT:    We're going to take these gentlemen down and put this in its place. This (*he hands the replacement picture to* PHILLIPS) as you can see, is an *Annunciation*. Perhaps, Phillips, you could give us a technical description of the panel.

PHILLIPS:    Well, it's constructed of two planks, joined by a horizontal brace . . .

BLUNT:    Two planks of what?

PHILLIPS:    Wood.

BLUNT:    Oak? Ash? Chipboard?

PHILLIPS:    It's probably poplar.

BLUNT:    Why?

PHILLIPS:    Because it generally is. (*He turns it over.*)

BLUNT:    So that's the back finished, is it? What about the frame?

PHILLIPS:    Gilt.

BLUNT:    Old gilt or modern gilt?

PHILLIPS:    I can't tell.

BLUNT:    Colin, any thoughts?

COLIN:    Modern, I'd have said. Relatively, anyway. Glazing generally well-preserved. Some worm but there seems to be very little retouching. Number of holes have been repaired, particularly round knots in the wood. It *is* poplar, actually. Some re-touching here, see. Minute flaking along the outline of the angel's robe. A few pentimenti visible to the naked eye, most clearly the fingers of the Virgin's left hand. Reserve judgement on the attribution, but a preliminary impression would suggest Siena.

BLUNT:    Good. Phillips, the steps. Colin, would you move the banquette.

(*He hasn't been listening but has been looking fixedly at the* Triple Portrait *on the wall.*)

Hold the steps. (*He ascends the steps.*) This painting was in the collection of Charles I where it was ascribed to Titian, and it hung with other, rather more plausible Titians in the palace at Whitehall.

(BLUNT *is addressing this speech to the painting while examining it closely. Meanwhile* COLIN *spots Someone approaching offstage right. He nudges* PHILLIPS, *indicating he should go.*)

COLIN:   Sir.

BLUNT:   Shut up. It was sold off after Charles I's execution but was recovered by Charles II and hung quite happily in the royal collection, nobody having any doubts about it at all until the end of the nineteenth century. Titian's beard is so badly done it looks as if it hooks on behind the ears.

(COLIN *and* PHILLIPS *hurriedly scarper, stage left. The stage is empty for a moment or two as* BLUNT *goes on talking to the picture.*)

One lesson to be learned from paintings as indifferent as this, is that there is no such thing as a royal collection. It is rather a royal accumulation.

(THE QUEEN *has entered, quite slowly. She looks. She is about to pass on.*)

Could you hand me my glass. (BLUNT *puts his hand down without looking.*) It's on the table. Come along—we haven't got all day.

(HMQ *thinks twice but then hands him his glass.*)

Thank you. I thought so. Where are my notes? (*He comes down, still with his back to* HMQ.) You're supposed to be holding the steps. I could have fallen flat on my face.

HMQ:   I think you already have.

BLUNT:   Your Majesty, I'm so sorry.

HMQ:   Not at all. One was most instructed. You were about to make a note.

BLUNT:   It can wait, Ma'am.

HMQ:   No. Carry on, do it now. Ignore me.

BLUNT:   Very well, Ma'am.

(HMQ *looks at the picture while* BLUNT *scribbles a note.*)

HMQ:   And how did we accumulate this particular picture?

BLUNT:   It belonged to Charles I, Ma'am.

HMQ:   King Charles I?

BLUNT:   Ma'am. It was thought to be by Titian.

HMQ:   And now it isn't?

BLUNT:   Not altogether, Ma'am.

HMQ:   I suppose that is part of your function, Sir Anthony, to prove that my pictures are fakes?

BLUNT:   Because something is not what it is said to be, Ma'am, does not mean it is a fake. It may just have been wrongly attributed.

HMQ:   Yes. It's a fine face, though he looks as if he could do with some fresh air. Who is he?

BLUNT:   His name is Andrea Franceschi. He was Chancellor of Venice.

HMQ:   We were in Venice two years ago. Unusual place. So. Now that it's a fake, what are you planning to do with it? Put it out for the binmen?

BLUNT:   A painting is a document, Ma'am. It has to be read in the context of art history.

HMQ:   Has art always had a history? It's all the thing now, isn't it, but one doesn't remember it when one was young. There was art appreciation.

BLUNT:   Art history is a part of art appreciation, Ma'am. We know that in this painting the old man is Titian himself, it's copied from one of his self-portraits, and that's the Chancellor of Venice, but this other gentleman is something of a mystery. I'm trying to identify him, and with your permission, Ma'am, I'd like to remove the painting to examine it at my leisure.

HMQ:   Remove it? I'm not sure I want that. It would leave us with a horrid hole.

BLUNT:   I have something to put in its place, Ma'am. (*Showing her the* Annunciation.) It's an *Annunciation*.

HMQ:   Yes, I know what it is.

BLUNT:   You're not attached to this particular picture, are you, Ma'am?

HMQ:   No, but it's there, you know. One's used to it.

BLUNT:   I think it was Gertrude Stein who said that after a while even the best pictures turn into wallpaper.

HMQ:   Really? This wallpaper is pure silk. I was shown some silkworms once, in Sri Lanka. It's their cocoons, you know.

BLUNT:   Yes. I had understood you weren't going to be here this afternoon.

HMQ:   Obviously. I had understood I wasn't going to be here, either. I was due to open a swimming bath. Completed on Friday, filled on Saturday, it cracked on Sunday and today it's as dry as a bone. So this afternoon one is, to some extent, kicking one's heels.

BLUNT:   That must make a nice change.

HMQ:   Not altogether. One likes to know in advance what one is going to be doing, even if one is going to be hanging about. If I am doing nothing, I like to be doing nothing to some purpose. That is what leisure means. (*She indicates an object on a table.*) This ostrich egg was given us by the people of Samoa. It hasn't quite found its place yet. (*Pause.*) Titian.

BLUNT:   Ma'am?

HMQ:   That isn't really your period, is it?

BLUNT:   In what way?

HMQ:   You are an expert on Poussin, are you not?

BLUNT:   That's right, Ma'am.

HMQ:   Chicken.

BLUNT:   Ma'am?

HMQ:   Poussin. French for chicken. One has just had it for lunch. I suppose it's fresh in the mind. It was one of what I call my All Walks of Life luncheons. Today we had the head of the CBI, an Olympic swimmer, a primary school headmistress, a General in the Salvation Army, and Glenda Jackson. It was a bit sticky.

BLUNT:   I've been to one, Ma'am. That was a bit sticky, too.

HMQ:   The trouble is, whenever I meet anybody they're always on their best behaviour. And when one is on one's best behaviour one isn't always at one's best. I don't understand it. They all have different jobs, there ought to be heaps to talk about, yet I'm always having to crank it up.

BLUNT:   The truth is, Ma'am, one doesn't have much to say to people very different from oneself. If you'd had the General in the Salvation Army, the Archbishop of Canterbury and the President of the Methodist Conference, they could all have talked about God, and lunch would have been a howling success.

HMQ:   Yes. And guess who would have been staring at her plate. And think if they were all actors.

BLUNT:   At least they would talk, Ma'am.

HMQ:   Correction, Sir Anthony. They wouldn't talk. They would chat. One doesn't want chat. I don't like chat.

BLUNT:   Weren't we chatting about Poussin, Ma'am?

HMQ:   Were we? Well, we mustn't. We must do it properly. Feed me facts, Sir Anthony. I like a fact. What were his dates?

BLUNT:   1595 to 1665.

HMQ:   Seventy. A good age for those days. How many pictures did he do?

BLUNT:   Er . . .

HMQ:   Don't you know?

BLUNT:   I've never been asked that before, Ma'am. He wasn't a prolific artist.

HMQ:   Have we got any?

BLUNT:   Paintings, no, Ma'am, but what you do have is a priceless collection of drawings.

HMQ:   Oh dear. So many of my things are priceless. Doubly so, really. Priceless because one can't put a price on them, and then if one did one wouldn't be allowed to sell them. Do you have pictures?

BLUNT:   One or two, Ma'am.

HMQ:   Are they valuable?

BLUNT:   Yes, but they are not invaluable. Though I do have a Poussin.

HMQ:   You mean you have one and we don't? Something wrong there.

BLUNT:   Do you take any pleasure in acquisition, Ma'am?

HMQ:   Why? I'm not asking you to make me a present of it. That was one of my grandmother's tricks, Queen Mary. Acquired no end of stuff.
    Accumulated it. But pleasure in buying things? No, I like buying horses, as everybody knows, but why not? I know about them.
    But you're right. One more Fabergé egg isn't going to make my day. Go on with your work. Don't let me stop you.

BLUNT:   It seems rude.

HMQ:   I'm used to it. My days are spent watching people work. My work is watching people work.

BLUNT:   Very well, Ma'am. (*He goes on making notes.*)

HMQ:   What is it you want to know about the painting?

BLUNT:   Many things. It's a problem picture.

HMQ:   Not to me. But then I don't suppose wallpaper can be a problem, can it? Where will you take it?

BLUNT:   The laboratory.

HMQ:   Oh dear. I don't know. But I'm inclined to say no. It's the constant *va et vient* of one's things. A monarch has been defined as someone who doesn't have to look behind them sitting down. No longer. One has to look round nowadays because the odds are the Chippendale is on exhibition somewhere. (*She picks up a bowl.*) This rose bowl was a wedding present from the people of Jersey.

BLUNT:   Do you still have all your wedding presents, Ma'am?

HMQ:   Not all. For instance, it was 1947. Clothes were still rationed. Result was, one was inundated with nylons. I don't still have them. Do you like it?

BLUNT:   Not altogether, Ma'am.

HMQ:   I do, quite. But then I've never set much store by taste. That, after all, is your job. In mine, taste isn't such a good idea. When one looks at my predecessors the monarchs with the best taste . . . I'm thinking of Charles I; and George III and IV . . . made a terrible hash of the rest of it. I don't think taste helps. Do you paint?

BLUNT:   I'm afraid not, Ma'am. I have no skill in that department.

HMQ:   Nor me. The Prince of Wales paints, and my husband. They both claim it is very soothing. As a child I found it the reverse. My colours always used to run. I like things to have a line round them.

BLUNT:   You must have had more experience of painters than most.

HMQ:   In what way?

BLUNT:   Through having your portrait painted.

HMQ:   Oh, that. Yes. Though one gets the impression that as artists portrait painters don't really count. Not nowadays anyway.

BLUNT:   They're seldom standard-bearers of the avant-garde, Ma'am.

HMQ:   They would hardly be painting me if they were. One doesn't want two noses. Mind you, that would make one no more unrecognizable than some of their efforts. No resemblance at all. Sometimes I think it would be simpler to send round to Scotland Yard for an Identikit. Still I can understand it when they get me wrong, but some of them get the horse wrong, too. That's unforgivable.

BLUNT:   It's true none of them quite capture you.

HMQ:   I hope not. I don't think one wants to be captured, does one? Not entirely, anyway.

BLUNT:   You sound like one of those primitive tribes who believe an image confers some power on the possessor.

HMQ:   If I believed that, Sir Anthony, I am in the pocket of anyone with a handful of change.

BLUNT:   Portrait painters tend to regard faces as not very still lives. There was one eminent portrait painter who said he wished he could hang his sitters upside down by the leg like a dead hare.

HMQ:   Yes. Well, one Minister of the Arts wanted to loose Francis Bacon on me, and that's probably how I would have ended up. He did the *Screaming Pope,* didn't he? I suppose I would have been the *Screaming Queen.*

(*He laughs. She doesn't. She picks up something else.*)

This is charming, isn't it. It's antelope horn. A gift from the National Association of Girls' and Mixed Clubs. Nowadays, of course, they don't even do sketches; they take photographs, then take them home and copy them. I think that's cheating.

BLUNT:   I'm sure Michelangelo would have used the camera, Ma'am, if it had been invented. And Leonardo would probably have invented it.

(*He smiles, but she doesn't.*)

HMQ:   You see, I would call doing it from a photograph, *tracing.* Art, to my mind, has to be what we used to call freehand drawing. If you paint it from a photograph one might as well have a photograph.

BLUNT:   The portrait everybody likes best does look like a photograph.

HMQ:   The Annigoni. I like that one too. Portraits are supposed to be frightfully self-revealing, aren't they, good ones. Show what one's really like. The secret self. Either that, or the eyes are supposed to follow you round the room. I don't know that one has a secret self. Though it's generally assumed that one has. If it could be proved that one hadn't, some of the newspapers would have precious little to write about. Have you had your portrait painted?

BLUNT:   No, Ma'am.

HMQ:   So we don't know whether you have a secret self.

BLUNT:   I think the only person who doesn't have a secret self, Ma'am, must be God.

HMQ:   Oh? How is that?

BLUNT:    There is no sense in which one could ask, 'What is God really like'? Never off duty—he must always be the same. It must make it very dull. There can be no gossip in Heaven.

HMQ:    Good. I don't like gossip. This clock shows the time not only here but also in Perth, Western Australia. In certain circumstances it could be quite handy. I suppose for me Heaven is likely to be a bit of a comedown. What about you?

BLUNT:    I'm not sure I'll get in, Ma'am.

HMQ:    Why on earth not? You've done nothing wrong. Your father was a clergyman, after all. Are all owners co-operative about lending their pictures?

BLUNT:    None as co-operative as yourself, Ma'am.

HMQ:    That is the kind of remark, Sir Anthony, were it in a play, to which one would reply 'Tush'!

BLUNT:    Truly, Ma'am.

HMQ:    Well, I think I'm going to blot my copybook on this one and persuade you to take St Sebastian instead.

BLUNT:    He wouldn't be much use to me, Ma'am.

HMQ:    Not much use to anybody. I find him faintly ludicrous. Turned into a human pincushion and he just looks as if it were a minor inconvenience.

BLUNT:    The saints tended to be like that, Ma'am. Though there's more excuse for St Sebastian as he didn't actually die of his wounds.

HMQ:    Oh. That was lucky.

BLUNT:    He survived and was flogged to death.

HMQ:    Oh dear. Out of the frying-pan into the fire. And what about this *Annunciation* you want to foist on to me? Where's it been? In the cellar?

BLUNT:    Hampton Court.

HMQ:    Same thing. What should I know about the *Annunciation?* Come along. Facts.

BLUNT:    The Virgin is traditionally discovered reading. It's quite amusing that as time went on, painters tended to elevate the status of the Holy Family, so that Joseph—from being a simple carpenter—eventually comes to be depicted as a full-blown architect; and the Virgin, who to begin with is just given a book, ends up with a reading desk and a whole library, so that in some later versions Gabriel looks as if he is delivering his message to the Mistress of Girton.

(HMQ *doesn't laugh.*)

HMQ:    Girton, Cambridge?

BLUNT:    Yes, Ma'am.

HMQ:    I opened them a new kitchen. Their gas cookers are among the most advanced in East Anglia. You see, one reason why I prefer that to this is that in a home (and this is a home, albeit only one of one's homes) one doesn't want too many pictures of what I would call a religious flavour. I mean, this isn't a church. Besides, this I think is rather unusual, whereas *Annunciations* are quite common. When we visited Florence we were taken round the Art Gallery there, and there—well, I won't say *Annunciations* are two a penny, but they certainly were quite thick on the ground. And not all of them very convincing. My husband remarked that one of them looked to him like the messenger arriving from Littlewood's Pools. And that the Virgin was protesting she had put a cross for no publicity. Fortunately, Signor de Gasperi's English was not good, or we should have had the Pope on our tracks. How long would you want it for, my Titian? My fake Titian.

BLUNT:    A few weeks.

HMQ:    Oh, very well. You see, what I don't like is the assumption that one doesn't notice, one doesn't care. Still, we're off to Zambia next week, so that will cushion the blow. One never stops, you know. Governments come and go. Or don't go. One never stops. Could I ask you a question, Sir Anthony? Have I many forgeries? What about these?

BLUNT:    Paintings of this date are seldom forgeries, Ma'am. They are sometimes not what we think they are, but that's different. The question doesn't pose itself in the form, 'Is this a fake'? so much as 'Who painted this picture and why'? Is it Titian, or a pupil or pupils of Titian? Is it someone who paints like Titian because he admires him and can't help painting in the same way? The public are rather tiresomely fascinated by forgery—more so, I'm afraid, than they are by the real thing.

HMQ:   Yes, well, as a member in this instance (somewhat unusually for me) of the public, I also find a forgery fascinating.

BLUNT:   Paintings make no claims, Ma'am. They do not purport to be anything other than paintings. It is we, the beholders, who make claims for them, attribute a picture to this artist or that.

HMQ:   With respect, Sir Anthony, rubbish. What if a painting is signed and the signature is a forgery?

BLUNT:   Forgery of that kind is much more a feature of modern or relatively modern paintings than of old masters, Ma'am.

HMQ:   Again, Sir Anthony, I find myself having to disagree with you. We were in Holland not long ago and after we had been taken to see the tulips and a soil structure laboratory, Queen Juliana showed us her Vermeers. One has a Vermeer, so one was quite interested.

BLUNT:   I think I know what you are going to say, Ma'am.

(THE QUEEN *gives him a sharp look.*)

. . . but please go ahead and say it.

HMQ:   Thank you, and (though you're obviously ahead of me) she showed us some of the forged Vermeers done by a Mr . . .

BLUNT:   Van Meegeren?

HMQ:   Quite. Those were forgeries. Of old masters.

BLUNT:   Ma'am is quite right.

HMQ:   Moreover, these Van Meegerens didn't seem to me to be the least bit like. Terrible daubs. God knows, one is no expert on Vermeer, but if I could tell they were fakes why couldn't other people see it at the time? When was it, in the forties?

BLUNT:   It's a complicated question, Ma'am.

HMQ:   Oh, don't spare me. Remember I could have been opening a swimming bath.

BLUNT:   What has exposed them as forgeries, Ma'am, is not any improvement in perception, but time. Though a forger reproduce in the most exact fashion the style and detail of his subject, as a painter he is nevertheless of his own time and however slavishly he imitates, he does it in the fashion of his time, in a way that is contemporary, and with the passage of years it is this element that dates, begins to seem old-fashioned, and which eventually unmasks him.

HMQ:   Interesting. I suppose too the context of the painting matters. Its history and provenance (is that the word?) confer on it a certain respectability. This can't be a forgery, it's in such and such a collection, its background and pedigree are impeccable—besides, it has been vetted by the experts . . . Isn't that how the argument goes? So if one comes across a painting with the right background and pedigree, Sir Anthony, then it must be hard, I imagine—even inconceivable—to think that it is not what it claims to be. And even supposing someone in such circumstances did have suspicions, they would be chary about voicing them. Easier to leave things as they are in every department. Stick to the official attribution rather than let the cat out of the bag and say, here we have a fake.

(*There is a strained pause.*)

BLUNT:   I still think the word 'fake' is inappropriate, Ma'am.

HMQ:   If something is not what it is claimed to be, what is it?

BLUNT:   An enigma?

HMQ:   That is, I think, the sophisticated answer. It's curious, Sir Anthony, but all the time we have been talking, there has been a young man skulking behind one of my Louis XV *bergères* (a gift from the de Gaulles). Do you think he is waiting to assassinate one, or does he have an interest in that particular *ébéniste*?

BLUNT:   My assistant, Ma'am.

HMQ:   I think it's time he was flushed from his lair. Come in, hiddy or not, young man.

(PHILLIPS *comes on left.*)

BLUNT:   This is Mr Phillips, Ma'am, a student at the Courtauld Institute.

PHILLIPS:   Your Majesty.

HMQ:   What do you plan to do with your art history?

PHILLIPS:   I am hoping to go into one of the big auction houses, Ma'am.

HMQ:   Jolly good. That should keep you out of mischief. Did you ever consider that, Sir Anthony?

BLUNT:   No, Ma'am.

HMQ:   Oh. Well, I must be on my way. Not, I think, a wasted afternoon. One has touched upon art, learned a little iconography, and something of fakes and forgery. Facts not chat. Of course, had I been opening the swimming bath I would have picked up one or two facts there: the pumping system; the filter process; the precautions against infectious diseases of the feet. All facts. One never knows when they may come in handy.

Be careful how you go up the ladder, Sir Anthony. One could have a nasty fall.

BLUNT:   Ma'am.

HMQ:   Mr Phillips. (HMQ *exits left.*)

PHILLIPS:   She seems quite on the ball.

BLUNT:   Oh, yes.

PHILLIPS:   The furniture, the pictures. I thought it was all horses.

(COLIN *enters left.*)

COLIN:   What the hell was madam doing here? What happened to the swimming bath?

PHILLIPS:   There was a leak.

COLIN:   I bet that made her shirty. They like their routine.

(*They are preparing to get the picture down.*)

BLUNT:   Strange about the Royal Family. They ask you a great deal but tell you very little.

COLIN:   What were you talking about?

BLUNT:   I was talking about art. I'm not sure that she was. Come on, let's get this bloody picture down.

BLUNT *watches as* COLIN *takes down the* Triple Portrait *and replaces it with the* Annunciation. *As* COLIN *carries off the* Triple Portrait *the Palace set disappears and* BLUNT, *pointer in hand, is once more found lecturing at the Courtauld Institute.*

BLUNT:   And should we compare these two paintings it is plain straightaway that they do not compare—at any rate in terms of quality. One, the *Allegory of Prudence,*

(*Slide of the* Allegory of Prudence [Figure 3].)

wholly authentic, Titian at the height of his powers, the other

(*Slide of the* Triple Portrait [Figure 2].)

a hotchpotch, a studio job, Titian's hand possibly to be detected in the striking central figure but nowhere else. But let us leave quality and authenticity aside while I direct your attention to two of the personages depicted.

(*A composite slide with Titian's son from the* Allegory of Prudence *on the left and the third man from the* Triple Portrait *on the right* [Figure 4].)

On the left, Titian's son Orazio Vecelli as he appears in the *Allegory of Prudence.* No doubt about him or his identity, and rather a bruiser he looks, like one of those extravagant villains in an early Chaplin film. On the right altogether more civilized, if not so well painted, is this gentleman.

Younger, perhaps, and with a beard which has not yet achieved its full tropical luxuriance, but with the same eyes, the same nose, surely this is the same man, Titian's son also. The identification has never been made, and I make it now only tentatively and, I hasten to say, to no larger purpose, because even if correct I cannot say it helps to solve the riddle of this picture—if indeed it is a riddle worth solving. But riddle there undoubtedly is as I shall show you. Let us look at the painting as it was when it first turns up in the collection of Charles I some three hundred and fifty years ago. Catalogued as *Titian and a Venetian Senator,* you will note that it then contained only two figures.

(*Slide of the* Triple Portrait *before cleaning* [Figure 1].)

When I was appointed Surveyor of the Queen's Pictures, I had the painting cleaned, and the presence of the mysterious gentleman on the right was revealed.

(*Slide of the* Triple Portrait *after cleaning* [Figure 2].)

So, having started with two men, we now have a third man. And that is how the picture looks at the moment. But that is only how it looks. Because in addition to being cleaned, I also had the picture X-rayed. And the X-ray revealed a fourth man.

(*Slide of an X-ray photograph of the* Triple Portrait [*as reproduced in the* Burlington *magazine, Volume 100, 1958*].)

And that was not the end of it either, for if we rotate the X-ray we find behind the original pair and the third and fourth man the rather more substantial figure of a fifth man.

(*Slide of the X-ray rotated.*)

The fifth man, you will doubtless be relieved to learn, is the last of the sitters lurking in the somewhat over-populated canvas.

Who all these figures are and who painted them we do not know. It may be that the third man is indeed Titian's son, but even so that does not help us identify the fourth man or the fifth. And why, you're entitled to ask, does it matter? This is not an important picture, just a murky corner of sixteenth-century art history that wants clearing up but won't be. It matters, I suggest to you as a warning.

(*Slide of* Triple Portrait [Figure 2].)

This painting is a riddle, and this and similar riddles are quests the art historian can pursue for years and indeed their solution is one of the functions of the art historian. But it is only *one* of his functions. Art history is seldom thought of as a hazardous profession. But a life spent teasing out riddles of this kind does carry its own risks . . . a barrenness of outlook, a pedantry that verges on the obsessive, and a farewell to common sense; the rule of the hobby horse. Because, though the solution might add to our appreciation of this painting, paintings—we must never forget—are not there primarily to be solved. A great painting will still elude us, as art will always elude exposition.

*(The transition from lecture hall to* BLUNT's *room begins as the light grows on* CHUBB, *in raincoat. He picks up a paper from* BLUNT's *desk and reads it.)*

CHUBB:   A long time ago when I first started, I thought . . . or thought that I thought . . . that art was in the front line. I used to review then. I was the art critic of *The Spectator* . . . and I sang the praises of realism from Rembrandt to Rivera, deplored Picasso and abstraction . . . inaccessible to the people, I suppose. What none of us I suppose realized then was that the people would mean the public to the extent it does today.

*(BLUNT enters. He is in full evening dress with the ribbons and medals of his various orders and decorations. He carries a bottle of whisky and two glasses.)*

What's this?

BLUNT:   My speech. The Academy Dinner.

CHUBB:   I hadn't planned on calling. I saw your light was on.

BLUNT:   Yes. I suppose it's what you'd call a function.

CHUBB:   Who was there?

BLUNT:   Oh, everybody. Including your boss. We chatted. Do you not get invited to occasions like that?

CHUBB:   No.

BLUNT:   You should.

CHUBB:   I'd feel a bit lost.

BLUNT:   Oh, I don't think so. They were all there.

CHUBB:   Who?

BLUNT:   The great and the good. Everybody on your list. Your little list.

CHUBB:   Anyway, I don't have the clothes.

BLUNT:   Clothes are the least of it. Your wife would like it. Plenty to goggle at. And in the absence of the public one can see the art. Drink?

CHUBB:   Thank you.

I came to give you a warning. There is a time coming, soon, when your anonymity will cease to be in any practical sense useful.

BLUNT:    Yes, yes, yes.

CHUBB:    You must understand that your situation does not improve with time. More and more questions are being asked. The wolves, if you like, are getting closer. We may have to throw you off our sledge now. The consequences will be embarrassing, and not only for you. For us too. It will be painful. You will be the object of scrutiny, explanations sought after, your history gone into. You will be named. Attributed.

BLUNT:    And as a fake I shall, of course, excite more interest than the genuine article.

CHUBB:    There is someone else. Someone behind you all. All the evidence points to it.

BLUNT:    The evidence! Once upon a time, when Berenson began his pioneer work of listing and attributing the paintings of the Italian Renaissance, he sometimes came across groups of works in which he detected a family resemblance. They pointed to the existence of artists to whom he could not give a name. And there was one group of drawings that resembled—but were not—the work of Botticelli. So he called the putative author of these drawings Amico di Sandro— the friend of Botticelli. But as the work of attribution progressed, Berenson came to see that these drawings were actually the early work of the Florentine painter Filippino Lippi. The point is there was no Amico di Sandro. Lippi had invented him to fit his evidence, but he did not exist.

CHUBB:    It's funny you should mention Berenson. I've just got on to him. Fascinating chap. Only wasn't there another group of paintings he was puzzled about? Of the Mother and Child? Same situation, they resembled one another in style but he couldn't put a name to the artist. The one element they all had in common was that the Christ child wasn't portrayed as the usual torpid, overweight infant but as a real, live wriggling baby. So this process of attribution called into being a painter Berenson called the Maestro del Bambino Vispo . . . the painter of the wriggling baby. I've not got very far in my studies in art history, of course, but, and you'll correct me if I'm wrong, but that attribution . . . the Maestro del Bambino Vispo still stands. He did exist.

BLUNT:   Yes. That's right. He did. But whether your man existed, or still exists, is a different matter. But very good. You might have made an art historian.

CHUBB:   Did I miss my way?

BLUNT:   Not really, though both our professions carry the same risks . . . a barrenness of outlook, a pedantry that verges on the obsessive, a farewell to commonsense, the rule of the hobby horse. You with your hobby horse, me with mine.

(CHUBB *punches up the X-ray of the fifth man.*)

CHUBB:   Who are they all?

BLUNT:   Oh no, not more photographs. I'm sorry. I thought they were yours, not mine. When I was in the security service art became a haven. A refuge. In the silly, knowing jargon of the spy story, a safe house. Only it's not so safe now. Everybody's into art.

CHUBB:   Including me.

BLUNT:   Still, I think it will last my time. But who are they all? (BLUNT *switches the slide off.*) What difference does it make? Behind them both lurk other presences, other hands. A whole gallery of possibilities. The real Titian an Allegory of Prudence. The false one an Allegory of Supposition. It is never-ending.

(CHUBB *and* BLUNT *sit spotlit for a moment before the lights fade.*)

# TALKING HEADS

# Contents

# Introduction

THESE SIX MONOLOGUES were written and recorded for television. Forms, one is often led to think, dictate themselves, the material demanding to be written in a particular way and no other. I would be happy to think this were so with these pieces, but I'm not sure it's true. A *Chip in the Sugar*, for instance, or *Bed Among the Lentils* could both have been written as plays proper. It would be fun to see Mr Turnbull, Mrs Whittaker's fancy man, in the flesh (and his three-quarter-length windcheater), or Mrs Shrubsole doing her ruthless flower arranging—see them for ourselves, that is, rather than through the eyes of Graham and Susan who narrate those respective stories. But then they would be different stories, more objective, rounded and altogether fairer to the people the narrator is talking about. None of these narrators after all is telling the whole story. Geoffrey, Susan's husband, may be a nicer, more forbearing man than her account of him might lead us to suppose; and Mr Turnbull may not be quite the common fellow ('could have been a bookie') the jealous Graham is so ready to disparage. And were these monologues plays, there would be room for qualification and extenuation, allowances could be made, redemptions hinted at, a different point of view. Instead there is a single point of view, that of the speaker alone with the camera, and with the rest of the story pictured and peopled by the viewer, more effort is demanded of the imagination. In this sense to watch a monologue on the screen is closer to reading a short story than watching a play.

Admittedly it is a stripped-down version of a short story, the style of its telling necessarily austere. 'Said' or 'says' is generally all that is required to introduce reported speech, because whereas the novelist or short story writer has a battery of expressions to choose from ('exclaimed', 'retorted', 'groaned', 'lisped'), in live narration such terms seem literary and self-conscious. Adverbs too ('she remarked, tersely') seem to over-egg the pudding or else acquire undue weight in the mouth of a supposedly artless narrator. And these narrators are artless. They don't quite know what they are saying and are telling a story to the meaning of which they are not entirely privy. In *A Chip in the Sugar* Graham would not accept that he is married to his mother, or Miss Ruddock in *A Lady of Letters* that she is not a public-spirited guardian of morals. In *Soldiering On* Muriel ends up knowing her husband ruined her daughter but is no closer to realising that she had a hand in it too. Lesley in *Her Big Chance* thinks she has a great deal to offer both as an actress and a person, and Susan, the vicar's wife in *Bed Among the Lentils*, doesn't realise it's not just the woman in the off-licence but the whole parish that knows she's on the drink. Only Doris, the old lady who has fallen and broken her hip in *A Cream Cracker Under the Settee*, knows the score and that she is done for, but though she can see it's her determination to dust that's brought about her downfall, what she doesn't see is that it's the same obsession that tidied her husband into the grave.

I am disturbed, as I was with a previous collection of television plays, to note so many repetitions and recurrences. There are droves of voluntary workers, umpteen officials from the social services, and should there be a knock on the door, it's most likely to be a bearded vicar. Even Emily Brontë turns up twice. If I'm guilty of repeating myself, on another count I plead innocence. The suspicion of child abuse in *A Lady of Letters* and the hint of it in *Soldiering On* might suggest I am straining after topicality. My instinct is generally to take flight in the opposite direction, and in fact both these pieces were written and recorded before the subject began regularly to hit the headlines. Since several of the characters fare badly at the hands of social and community workers, I might seem to be taking a currently fashionable line here also. In the popular press nowadays social workers are generally (and easily) abused. I have little experience of them and to seem to line up with the *Sun* or the *Daily Express* would dismay me. My quarrel with social work is not with its praiseworthy practicalities but with the jargon in which it's sometimes conducted. Graham's 'I am not being defensive about sexual intercourse; she is my mother' is a protest about language.

Some of the events in these stories stem from actual occurrences in my life, though they are often joined to it by a very narrow isthmus. The funeral with which *Soldiering On* begins (though none of the characters in it) was suggested by the funeral of the composer George Fenton's father, who had been in Colditz and like Ralph had touched life at many points. Though much of the church stuff in *Bed Among the Lentils* (including Mr Medlicott the verger) comes from my childhood, the disaffection of Susan, the vicar's wife, I can trace to opening a hymn book in the chapel of Giggleswick School and finding in tiny, timid letters on the fly leaf, 'Get lost, Jesus'. Of these six characters only Lesley, the small-part actress, is wholly modern (while being quite old-fashioned). She and dozens like her have auditioned for films and plays I've done in the last twenty years. One of the first Lesley-like characters was a boy who came up for a part in *Forty Years On*. The director asked him what he had done:

'I was in George Bernard Shaw'.

'What did you play'?

'The drums'.

Perky, undefeated, their hopes of stardom long since gone, these actors retail the films and plays one might have glimpsed them in, playing waiters or barmen or, like Lesley, travelling on the back of a farm cart next to the star, wearing a shawl, the shawl 'original nineteenth-century embroidery, all hand done'. I saw an actor for a part not long ago who had been in a few episodes of *Emmerdale Farm*. 'I played the postman', he said, 'only I haven't done any since. They don't seem to be getting much mail'.

Another obsession goes back to childhood. The dog dirt outside Buckingham Palace that spoils Miss Ruddock's Awayday and the 'little hairs all up and down' that rule out a dog for Doris betray a prejudice inherited from my father. He was plagued by dogs: 'Get out, you nasty lamppost-smelling little article', he shouted once as he raced some unfortunate mongrel from his butcher's shop, and now thirty years later Doris has the line. It was my father too who had a craze for fretwork, but whereas for Doris's husband Wilfred fretwork is just one of his dreams ('toys and forts and whatnot, no end of money he was going to make'), with Dad it was no dream. Sitting at his little treadle saw with plans from *Hobbies Magazine* beside him, he made forts and farms for my brother and me, a toy butcher's shop once and wonderfully elaborate constructions of ramps and trapdoors into which we shot marbles. This was at the start of the Second War when toys were scarce, and for a few years he was able to make a little money selling some of his stuff to a toyshop down County Arcade off Briggate. It wasn't much though. 'You want to ask a bit more', my mam used to say. 'They take advantage of you. That's your trouble, Walt, you won't push yourself'. Which sounds like Doris again. Toy penguins were Dad's speciality, made out of three-ply and set on a behind, scanning the face of its small owner for any evidence of pleasure in this (to me very dull) toy, Dad presumably experiencing some of the same pleasure a writer gets when he catches someone reading his book.

It's with mixed feelings that I see tattoos are (twice) sniffed at, along with red paint, yellow gloves and two-tone cardigans. These disparagements too date back to home and childhood, where they were items in a catalogue of disapproval that ranged through (fake) leopardskin coats, dyed (blonde) hair to slacks, cocktail cabinets and statuettes of ladies with alsatian dogs on leash. In our house and in my mother's idiosyncratic scheme of things, they were all common. Common is not an easy term to define without seeming to brand the user as snobbish or socially pretentious, which my mother wasn't. But it was always her distinction: I never remember my father making it, and both in its use and application common tended to be a woman's term. 'She's a common woman' one heard more often (was more common) than 'He's a common feller', perhaps because in those days women had more time and inclination to make such distinctions. A common woman was likely to swear or drink (or drink 'shorts'), to get all dolled up and go out leaving the house upside down and make no bones about having affairs. Enjoy herself, possibly, and that was the trouble; a common woman sidestepped her share of the proper suffering of her sex. What was also being criticised was an element of pretension and display (the dyed blonde hair, the too-tight slip-over, the face plastered with make-up). Elsie Tanner was a common woman, as with her curlers and too ready opinions is Hilda Ogden. And so, I thought as a child, was Mary Magdalen.

Sudden money augmented the risk, and pools winners would find it hard to avoid the epithet. Hence the unfortunate tale of Vivien Nicholson, the Yorkshire pools winner and heroine of Jack Rosenthal's *Spend, Spend, Spend*. Her persistent car crashes and the dramas and notorieties of her personal life were never out of the *Evening Post*. 'Well', my mother used to say, as Mrs N wrote off yet another of her cars and her lovers in some frightful motorway pile-up, 'she's a common woman'. No other explanation was necessary.

Places could be common too, particularly at the seaside. Blackpool was common (people enjoying themselves), Morecambe less so (not enjoying themselves as much), and Grange or Lytham not common at all (enjoyment not really on the agenda). If we ever did get to Blackpool we stayed at Cleveleys or Bispham, the refined end. To my brother and me (and I suspect to the local estate agents) refined just meant furthest away from the funfair. Not that where we stayed made much difference to the type of boarding house or the mixed bag we found there. To some extent my mother's nice distinctions were subjective and self-fulfilling: we met a better class of person where we stayed because we kept out of the way of the rest, Palm Court rather than bathing beauties, not the knobbly knees contest but a Wallace Arnold to Windermere. Package holidays came too late for my parents, but had they ever ventured abroad they would have taken their attitudes with them. My mam would soon have located the Bispham end of Benidorm, a select part to Sitges. 'Well, we don't like it all hectic, do we, Dad'?

Common persists. It's not a distinction I'd want to be detected making, but to myself I make it still. There are some lace (or more likely nylon) curtains popular nowadays that are gathered up for some reason in the middle. They look to me like a woman who's been to the lav and got her underskirt caught up behind her. They're absurd, but that's not my real objection. They're common. The mock Georgian doorways that disfigure otherwise decent houses, the so-called Kentucky-fried Georgian, offend me because they're cheap, inappropriate, ill-proportioned . . . and common.

Finally vicars who, Anglican though not always specified as such, turn up in all but one of these pieces, earnest, visitant and resolutely contemporary. Several are bearded, one is in trainers and most are in mufti. I have no particular wish to lock the clergy out of the wardrobe or ban them the boutique, but along with postmen and porters I wish they had not abandoned black. Just as postmen nowadays look like members of the Rumanian airforce, so cassocks come in beige and even lilac, and if a parson submits to the indignity of a dog collar the chances are it has gone slimline, peeping coyly above a modish number in some fetching pastel shade. Nuns too have lost their old billowing, wimpled innocence and now look like prison wardresses on the loose. Even hearses have gone grey, black altogether too uncompromising a colour, life something to be shaded out of when, after much suffering tastefully borne, we blend nicely into the grave.

The clergy not wanting to look the part has something to do with the dismantling of the Book of Common Prayer. Anxious not to sound like parsons they can hardly be blamed for not wanting to look like them either. The 'underneath this cassock I am but a man like any other' act that Geoff does in *Bed Among the Lentils* must be a familiar routine at many a church door. And it's not of course new. Priests have always hankered after the world, or at any rate the worldly, and consorting as He did with publicans and sinners, it was Jesus who started the rot. Or so Susan would say.

I don't know why it should be only Catholics who are thought never to escape their religious upbringing; I have never managed to outgrow mine. When I was sixteen and not long confirmed I was devoutly religious, a regular communicant who knew the service off by heart. It might be thought this would rejoice a vicar's heart and maybe it did, but actually I think the parish clergy found my fervour faintly embarrassing. A fervent Anglican is a bit of a contradiction in terms anyway, but I was conscious that my constant presence at the Eucharist, often midweek as well as Sundays, was thought to be rather unhealthy. As the celebrant sallied forth from the vestry on a cold winter's morning and found me sitting or (like Miss Frobisher, never one to let an opportunity slip) getting in a spot of silent prayer, he must have felt like a doctor opening the surgery door and discovering the sole occupant of the waiting room some tiresome hypochondriac (I was that too actually). Shy, bespectacled and innocent of the world, I knew I was a disappointment to the clergy. What they wanted were brands to pluck from the burning, and that was not me by a long chalk; I'd never even been near the fire.

Those early morning services with just a handful of regulars in the side chapel, the others generally maiden ladies who had cycled there on tall bicycles through the autumn mists, were to me the stuff of religion, the real taste of God. But though I did not admit it myself, I knew that what the clergy preferred were occasions like Christmas Eve when the church was packed to the doors, the side aisles full, people even standing at the back like they did in those days at the cinema. For many in the congregation this was their one visit to church in the year. Plumping to my knees with split-second timing I would scornfully note how few of these festive communicants knew the service. Most of them didn't even kneel but sat, head in hand as if they were on the lavatory, this their one spiritual evacuation of the year.

Fastidious worshipper that I was, when I got to the altar rail I was even more choosy, caring very much whom I knelt beside, though for reasons of hygiene rather than religion. At the sparsely attended Eucharists that were the norm for most of the year one could bank on finding oneself at the communion rail next to another regular, a spinster of proven piety, say, or a gentleman of blameless life. It's true that as my turn came for the chalice I might think of the TB or the cancer I could catch, but these ailments were as nothing to the risks one ran at the great services of Christmas or Easter. These joyous festivals of the Christian year figured in my calendar not as an occasion for rejoicing but as fearful health hazards and thus a true test of faith. I refer, of course, to VD, a real likelihood at Christmas, it seemed to me, when the church was so chock-a-block with publicans and sinners that one never knew who was going to be one's drinking companion.

It was all my mother's fault. She had brought us up never to share a lemonade bottle with other boys, and wiping it with your hand, she said, was no protection, so I knew the dainty dab with the napkin the priest gave the chalice made no difference at all. There was God of course, in whose omnipotence I was supposed to believe: He might run to some mystical antisepsis. But then He might not. That I should catch syphilis from the chalice might be all part of His plan. The other place I was frightened of contracting it was the seat of a public lavatory, and that the rim of the toilet should be thus linked with the rim of the chalice was also part of the wonderful mystery of God. It was on such questions of hygiene rather than any of theology that my faith cut its teeth. I see myself walking back from the altar and plunging to my knees, then at the first opportunity surreptitiously spitting into my handkerchief. But I knew that if God had marked me down for VD and a test of faith, no amount of spitting was going to help. It was all chickenfeed to the Ancient of Days.

Switching on the Test Match at Headingley by mistake nowadays, I see the scene of these early spiritual struggles. 'Why, Headingley'! I might say, parodying Larkin, 'I was re-born here'. The camera pans along the Cardigan Road boundary, and there above the trees is the spire of St Michael's, designed by J. L. Pearson who built Truro Cathedral, St Michael's with St Bartholomew's at Armley the best of the nineteenth-century churches in Leeds, and in those days I knew them all. Around the time I was spitting into my handkerchief David Storey, the novelist and playwright, was playing rugby for Wakefield and so was often on the Headingley ground. For him too St Michael's was a symbol of hope. Cold, wet and frightened in the middle of a game he would look longingly at the spire and tell himself that within the hour he would be stood opposite the church waiting for a tram; the match would be over and he would be going home. That is by the way, but then so is much of this reminiscence, my childhood itself fairly by the way, or so it seemed at the time. Brought up in the provinces in the forties and fifties one learned early the valuable lesson that life is generally something that happens elsewhere.

GRAHAM: ALAN BENNETT

# A Chip in the Sugar

*Graham is a mild middle-aged man. The play is set in his
bedroom, a small room with one window and one door. It
is furnished with a single bed, a wardrobe, two chairs and
nothing much else.*

I'd just taken her tea up this morning when she said, 'Graham, I
think the world of you'. I said, 'I think the world of you'. And she said,
'That's all right then'. I said, 'What's brought this on'? She said,
'Nothing. This tea looks strong, pull the curtains'. Of course I knew
what had brought it on. She said, 'I wouldn't like you to think you're
not Number One'. So I said, 'Well, you're Number One with me
too. Give me your teeth. I'll swill them'.

What it was we'd had a spot of excitement yesterday: we ran into a
bit of Mother's past. I said to her, 'I didn't know you had a past. I
thought I was your past'. She said, 'You'? I said, 'Well, we go back a
long way. How does he fit in vis-à-vis Dad'? She laughed. 'Oh, he
was pre-Dad'. I said, 'Pre-Dad? I'm surprised you remember him,
you don't remember to switch your blanket off'. She said, 'That's
different. His name's Turnbull'. I said, 'I know. He said'.

I'd parked her by the war memorial on her usual seat while I went
and got some reading matter. Then I waited while she went and spent
a penny in the disabled toilet. She's not actually disabled, her
memory's bad, but she says she prefers their toilets because you get
more elbow room. She always takes for ever, diddling her hands and
what not, and when she eventually comes back it turns out she's been
chatting to the attendant. I said, 'What about'? She said, 'Hanging.
She was in favour of stiffer penalties for minor offences and I thought,
"Well, we know better, our Graham and me". I wish you'd been
there, love; you could have given her the statistics, where are we
going for our tea'?

The thing about Mam is that though she's never had a proper
education, she's picked up enough from me to be able to hold her

87

own in discussions about up-to-the-minute issues like the environment and the colour problem, and for a woman of her age and background she has a very liberal slant. She'll look at my *Guardian* and she actually thinks for herself. Doctor Chaudhury said to me, 'Full marks, Graham. The best way to avoid a broken hip is to have a flexible mind. Keep up the good work'.

They go mad round the war memorial so when we cross over I'll generally slip my arm through hers until we're safely across, only once we're on the pavement she'll postpone letting it go, because once upon a time we got stopped by one of these questionnaire women who reckons to take us for husband and wife. I mean, Mam's got white hair. She was doing this dodge and I said, 'Mam, let go of my arm'. I didn't really wrench it, only next thing I knew she's flat on the pavement. I said, 'Oh my God, Mother'.

People gather round and I pick up her bag, and she sits up and says, 'I've laddered both my stockings'. I said, 'Never mind your stockings, what about your pelvis'? She says, 'It's these bifocals. They tell you not to look down. I was avoiding some sick'. Somebody says, 'That's a familiar voice', and there's a little fellow bending over her, green trilby hat, shorty raincoat. 'Hello', he says, 'remember me'?

Well, she doesn't remember people, I know for a fact because she swore me down she'd never met Joy Buckle, who teaches Flowers in Felt and Fabric at my day centre. I said, 'You have met Joy, you knitted her a tea cosy'. That's all she can knit, tea cosies. And bed socks. Both outmoded articles. I said to her, 'Branch out. If you can knit tea cosies you can knit skiing hats'. She says, 'Well, I will'. Only I have to stand over her or else she'll still leave a hole for the spout. 'Anyway', I said, 'you do remember Joy because you said she had some shocking eyebrows'. She said, 'I hope you didn't tell her that'. I said, 'Of course I didn't'. She said, 'Well, I don't remember'. And that's the way she is, she doesn't remember and here's this little fellow saying, 'Do you remember me'? So I said, 'No she won't. Come on, Mother. Let's get you up'. Only she says, 'Remember you? Of course. It's Frank Turnbull. It must be fifty years'. He said, 'Fifty-two. Filey. 1934'. She said, 'Sea-Crest'. He said, 'No sand in the bedrooms'. And they both cracked out laughing.

Meanwhile she's still stuck on the cold pavement. I said, 'Come along, Mother. We don't want piles'. Only he butts in again. He says, 'With respect, it's advisable not to move a person until it's been ascertained no bones are broken. I was in the St John's Ambulance Brigade'. 'Yes', said Mother, 'and who did you learn your bandaging on'? And they both burst out laughing again. He had on these bright yellow gloves, could have been a bookie.

Eventually, I get my arms round her waist and hoist her up, only his lordship's no help as he claims to have a bad back. When I've finally got her restored to the perpendicular she introduces him. 'This is Frank Turnbull, a friend of mine from the old days'. What old days? First time I knew there were any old days. Turns out he's a gents' outfitter, semi-retired, shop in Bradford and some sort of outlet in Morecambe. I thought, 'Well, that accounts for the yellow gloves'.

Straight off he takes charge. He says, 'What you need now, Vera, is a cup of coffee'. I said, 'Well, we were just going for some tea, weren't we, Mother'? Vera! Her name's not Vera. She's never been called Vera. My Dad never called her Vera, except just once, when they were wheeling him into the theatre. Vera. 'Right', he says, 'follow me'. And puts his arm through hers. 'Careful', she says. 'You'll make my boy friend jealous'. I didn't say anything.

*Pause.*

Now the café we generally patronise is just that bit different. It's plain but it's classy, no cloths on the tables, the menu comes on a little slate and the waitresses wear their own clothes and look as if they're doing it just for the fun of it. The stuff's all home-made and we're both big fans of the date and walnut bread. I said, 'This is the place'. Mr Turnbull goes straight past. 'No', he says, 'I know somewhere, just opened. Press on'.

Now, if there's one thing Mother and me are agreed on it's that red is a common colour. And the whole place is done out in red. Lampshades red. Waitresses in red. Plates red, and on the tables those plastic sauce things got up to look like tomatoes. Also red. And when I look there's a chip in the sugar. I thought, 'Mother won't like this'. 'Oh', she says, 'this looks cheerful, doesn't it, Graham'? I said, 'There's a chip in the sugar'. 'A detail', he says, 'they're still having their teething troubles. Is it three coffees'? I said, 'We like tea', only Mother says, 'No. I feel like an adventure. I'll have coffee'. He gets hold of the menu and puts his hand on hers. 'Might I suggest', he says, 'a cheeseburger'? She said, 'Oh, what's that'? He said, 'It's fresh country beef, mingled with golden-fried onions, topped off with toasted cheese served with french fries and lemon wedge'. 'Oh, lemon wedge', said Mother. 'That sounds nice'. I thought, 'Well, I hope you can keep it down'. Because it'll be the pizza story all over again. One mouthful and at four o'clock in the morning I was still stuck at her bedside with the bucket. She said, 'I like new experiences in eating. I had a pizza once, didn't I, Graham'? I didn't say anything.

They fetch the food and she's wiring in. He said, 'Are you enjoying your cheeseburger'? She said, 'I am. Would I be mistaken in thinking that's tomato sauce'? He said, 'It is'. She says, 'Give us a squirt'. They both burst out laughing. He said, 'Glass cups, Graham. Be careful or we'll see up your nose'. More laughter. She said, 'Graham's quite refined. He often has a dry sherry'.

'Well, he could do with smartening up a bit', Mr Turnbull said. 'Plastic mac. He wants one of these quilted jobs, I've shifted a lot of those'. 'I don't like those quilted jobs', I said. 'He sweats', Mother said. 'There's no excuse for that in this day and age', Mr Turnbull said, 'the range of preparations there are on the market. You want to invest in some roll-on deodorant'. Everybody could hear. 'And flares are anathema even in Bradford'.

'Graham doesn't care, do you, Graham'? Mother said. 'He reads a lot'. 'So what'? Mr Turnbull said. 'I know several big readers who still manage to be men about town. Lovat green's a nice shade. I tell you this, Graham', he said, 'if I were squiring a young lady like this around town I wouldn't do it in grey socks and sandals. These shoes are Italian. Feel'. 'I always think Graham would have made a good parson', Mother said, feeling his foot, 'only he doesn't believe in God'. 'That's no handicap these days', Mr Turnbull said. 'What do you do'?

'He's between jobs at present', Mother said. 'He used to do soft toys for handicapped children. Then he was making paper flowers at one stage'. I went to the toilet.

*Pause.*

When I came back he said, 'I don't believe in mental illness. Nine times out of ten it's a case of pulling your socks up'. I didn't say anything. Mother said, 'Yes, well, I think the pendulum's gone too far'. She didn't look at me. 'It's like these girls, not eating', he said, 'they'd eat if they'd been brought up like us, Vera, nothing to eat'. 'That's right', Mother said, 'they have it too easy. Did you marry'? 'Twice', he said. 'I buried Amy last May. I was heartbroken but life has to go on. I've a son lives in Stevenage. I've got two grandsons, one at the motorbike stage. Do you drive'? 'No', I said. 'You do', Mother said. 'You had that scooter'. 'It was only a moped', I said. 'Well, a moped, Graham. They're all the same. I can't get him to blow his own trumpet'.

'I've got a Rover 2000', Mr Turnbull said, 'handles like a dream. I think the solution to mental illness is hard physical work. Making raffia mats, I'd go mad'. 'Yes', says Mother, 'only they do pottery as well. I've seen some nice ashtrays'. 'Featherbedding', Mr Turnbull said. 'Do you like these Pakistanis'? 'Well, in moderation', Mother said. 'We have a nice newsagent. Graham thinks we're all the same'. I said, 'I thought you did'. She said, 'Well, I do when you explain it all to me, Graham, but then I forget the explanation and I'm back to square one'. 'There is no explanation', Mr Turnbull said. 'They sell mangoes in our post office, what explanation is there for that'? 'I know', Mother said, 'I smelled curry on my *Woman's Own*. You have to be educated to understand'. I didn't say anything.

He ran us home, promised to give her a tinkle next time he was in the neighbourhood. Said he was often round here tracking down two-tone cardigans. 'Your Mother's a grand woman', he said. 'You want to cherish her'. 'He does, he does', Mother said. 'You're my boy friend, aren't you, Graham'? She put her arm through mine.

*Go to black.*

*Come up on Graham standing looking out of the window.*
*It is late afternoon. He sits on the arm of the chair.*

There must be a famine on somewhere because we were just letting our midday meal go down when the vicar calls with some envelopes. Breezes in, anorak and running shoes, and he says, 'I always look forward to coming to this house, Mrs Whittaker'. (He's got the idea she's deaf, which she's not; it's one of the few things she isn't.) He says, 'Do you know why? It's because you two remind me of Jesus and his mother'. Well, I've always thought Jesus was a bit off-hand with his mother, and on one occasion I remember he was quite snotty with her, but I didn't say anything. And of course Madam is over the moon. In her book if you can't get compared with the Queen Mother the Virgin Mary's the next best thing. She says, 'Are you married'? (She asks him every time, never remembers.) He said, 'No, Mrs Whittaker. I am married to God'. She says, 'Where does that leave you with the housework'? He said, 'Well, I don't do as well as your Graham. He's got this place like a palace'. She says, 'Well, I do my whack. I washed four pairs of stockings this morning'. She hadn't. She put them in the bowl then they slipped her mind, so the rest of the operation devolved on me.

He said, 'How are you today, Mrs Whittaker'? She says, 'Stiff down one side'. I said, 'She had a fall yesterday'. She says, 'I never did'. I said, 'You did, Mother. You had a fall, then you ran into Mr Turnbull'.

*Pause.*

She says, 'That's right. I did'. And she starts rooting in her bag for her lipstick. She says, 'That's one of them anoraky things, isn't it? They've gone out now, those. If you want to look like a man about town you want to get one of those continental quilts'. He said, 'Oh'? I said, 'She means those quilted jackets'. She said, 'He knows what I mean. Where did you get those shoes'? He said, 'They're training shoes'. She said, 'Training for what? Are you not fully qualified'? He said, 'If Jesus were alive today, Mrs Whittaker, I think you'd find these were the type of shoes he would be wearing'. 'Not if his mother had anything to do with it', she said. 'She'd have him down Stead and Simpson's and get him into some good brogues. Somebody was telling me the Italians make good shoes'.

The vicar takes this as his cue to start on about people who have no shoes at all and via this to the famine in Ethiopia. I fork out 50p which he says will feed six families for a week and she says, 'Well, it would have bought me some Quality Street'. When he's at the door he says, 'I take my hat off to you, Graham, I've got a mother myself'. When I get back in she said, 'Vicar! He looked more like the paper boy. How can you look up to somebody in pumps'? Just then there's a knock at the door. 'Get down', she says, 'he's back'. Only it isn't. It's Mr Turnbull.

*Graham stands up.*

New outfit this time: little suede coat, corduroy collar, maroon trousers. She says, 'You're colourful'. 'We just happen to have these slacks on offer', he says. 'I was wondering whether you fancied a run out to Bolton Abbey'? 'Bolton Abbey'? she says. 'Oh, that's right up our street, isn't it, Graham? Graham's good with buildings, aren't you, Graham? He knows all the periods of houses. There's one period that's just come in. Other people don't like it yet but we do, don't we, Graham'? 'I don't know', I said. 'You do. What is it'? 'Victorian', I said. 'That's it, Victorian. Only there's a lot been pulled down'. Mr Turnbull yawns. 'I've got a little bungalow'. 'That's nice', Mother says. 'I like a nice bungalow, don't you, Graham'? 'Yes', I said, 'provided it's not a blot on the landscape'. 'Mine's architect designed', says Mr Turnbull. 'It has a patio and a breakfast bar, it overlooks a beauty spot'. 'Oh', said Mother, 'sounds tip-top. We'd better be getting our skates on, Graham'. He said, 'I've got to pick up a load of green three-quarter-length windcheaters in Ilkley; there won't really be room for a third party. Isn't there anything on at the pictures'? 'Oh he'll be happy reading', Mother said. 'Won't you, Graham'? 'Anyway', Mr Turnbull said, 'you don't always want to be with your Mother at your age, do you, Graham'? I didn't say anything.

*He sits on the chair arm again.*

I've been laid on my bed reading one of my magazines. I've a feeling that somebody's looking at the house, only I can't see anybody. Once or twice I think I've heard a knock on the door, but I haven't gone in case there's nobody there.

*Go to black.*

*Come up on Graham sitting on his unmade bed in his pyjamas. Night.*

Today they went over to York. It was after seven when he dropped her off. He generally comes in but not this time. Just gives her a little kiss. She has to bend down. I said, 'Have you had a good time'? She said, 'Yes. We had egg and chips, tea, bread and butter, we've got a lot in common and there's a grand new car park'. I said, 'Did you go in the Minster'? She said, 'No. Frank's not keen on old buildings. We need to look more to the future. He says they've built a spanking new precinct in Bradford, so that's going to be next on the agenda. You're quiet'. I said, 'Well, do you wonder? Doctor Chaudhury says I should have a stable environment. This isn't a stable environment with your fancy men popping in every five minutes'. She said, 'He isn't my fancy man'. I said, 'Well, he's your fancy man in embryo'. She said, 'You know I don't know what that means'. I said, 'How old are you'? She said, 'I don't know'. I said, 'You do know'. She said, 'I don't. Tell me'. I said, 'You're seventy-two'. 'That's not so old. How old was Winston Churchill'? I said, 'When'? She said, 'You think you've got it over me, Graham Whittaker. Well, I'll tell you something, my memory's better with Frank. He was telling me about the economy. You've got it all wrong'. I said, 'How'? 'I can't remember but you have. Blaming it on the government. Frank says it's the blacks'. I didn't say anything, just came upstairs.

When I went down again she's still sat there with her hat and coat on. I said: 'Do you want to knit him a tea cosy'? She said, 'I don't think he's the tea-cosy type. When I first knew him he had a motorbike and sidecar. Besides, I think it's got beyond the tea-cosy stage'. I said, 'What do you mean'? She said, 'Graham. My one aim in life is for you to be happy. If I thought that by dying I would make you happy I would'. I said, 'Mother, your dying wouldn't make me happy. In fact the reverse. It would make me unhappy. Anyway, Mother, you're not going to die'. She said, 'No. I'm not going to die. I'm going to get married. And the honeymoon is in Tenerife. Have one of your tablets'.

She made a cup of tea. I said, 'How can you go to Tenerife, you're smothered at Scarborough'? She said, 'It's a four-star hotel with tip-top air-conditioning, you get your breakfast from a long table'. I said, 'What about your bowels'? She said, 'What about my bowels'? 'Well, you said they were unpredictable at Morecambe. Get them to the Canary Islands and they're going to be all over the place'. She said, 'Who's talking about the Canary Islands? I'm going to Tenerife'. 'And what about post-Tenerife? Where are you going to live'? She said, 'Here. Frank says he'll be away on and off on business but he wants to call this home'. I said, 'What about me'? She went into the kitchen. 'Well, we wondered whether you'd prefer to go back to the hostel. You were happy at the hostel. You rubbed shoulders with all sorts'. I said, 'Mam. This is my home'. She said, 'A man shouldn't be living with his mother at your age, Frank says. Did you take a tablet'?

Now it's four o'clock in the morning and I can't sleep. There's a car parked outside. I can't see but I think there's somebody in it, watching like they used to do before. I thought all that chapter was closed.

*Go to black.*

*Come up on Graham sitting on an upright chair. Evening.*

This morning I went to Community Caring down at the Health Centre. It caters for all sorts. Steve, who runs it, is dead against what he calls 'the ghetto approach'. What he's after is a nice mix of personality difficulties as being the most fruitful exercise in problem-solving and a more realistic model of society generally. There's a constant flow of coffee, 'oiling the wheels' Steve calls it, and we're all encouraged to ventilate our problems and generally let our hair down. I sometimes feel a bit out of it as I've never had any particular problems, so this time when Steve says 'Now chaps and chappesses who's going to set the ball rolling'? I get in quick and tell them about Mother and Mr Turnbull. When I'd finished Steve said, 'Thank you, Graham, for sharing your problem with us. Does anybody want to kick it around'?

First off the mark is Leonard, who wonders whether Graham has sufficiently appreciated that old people can fall in love and have meaningful relationships generally, the same as young people. I suppose this is understandable coming from Leonard because he's sixty-five, only he doesn't have meaningful relationships. He's been had up for exposing himself in Sainsbury's doorway. As Mother said, 'Tesco, you could understand it'.

Then Janice chips in. 'Had they been having sexual intercourse'? I said I didn't want to think about it. Steve said, 'Why'? I said I didn't know. So he said, 'Maybe what we should be talking about is why Graham is being so defensive about sexual intercourse'. I said, 'Steve. I am not being defensive about sexual intercourse. She is my mother'. Jackie, who's nine parts Lesbian, said, 'Graham. She is also A Woman'. I couldn't believe this. I said, 'Jackie. You're an ex-battered wife. I thought you didn't approve of marriage'. She said, 'Graham. I approve of caring marriage'. I said, 'Jackie. This is not caring marriage'. She said, 'Graham, what's Tenerife? That's caring. All I got was a black eye and a day trip to Fleetwood'. Then they all have a go. Get Graham. Steve summed up. 'The general feeling of the group is that Graham could be more open'. I said, 'How can I be more open? There's somebody sat outside the house watching'. I wanted to discuss that only Leonard leaped in and said he felt the need to talk through an episode behind British Home Stores. I stuck it a bit longer and then came home.

Mother's sat there, all dolled up. Earrings on, chiffon scarf, lathered in make-up. She said, 'Oh, I thought you were Mr Turnbull'. I said, 'No'. She said, 'I'll just go to the lav'. She goes three times in the next ten minutes. I said, 'You're not getting married today, are you'? She said, 'No. There's a new Asda superstore opened at Bingley and we thought we'd give it the once over. Frank says they have a very good selection of sun tan lotions'. I said, 'Mother, there's somebody watching the house'. She said, 'I want to pick out some tissues and Frank's looking for a little chammy for his windscreen. He's promised me something called a cheeseburger, there's a café that's part of the complex'.

Just then there's a little toot on the horn and she runs to the lav again. I said, 'Don't go. Don't leave me, Mam'. She said, 'I'm not giving in to you, you're a grown man. Is my underskirt showing'? He toots again. She says, 'Look at your magazines, make yourself a poached egg'. I said, 'Mam'. She said, 'There's that bit of chicken in the fridge. You could iron those two vests. Take a tablet. Give us a kiss. Toodle pip'.

I thought I'd go sit in the back room where they couldn't see me. I pulled the curtains and I'm sitting there in the dark and I think I hear a knock at the front door. I don't move and there's another knock. Louder. I do like Doctor Chaudhury says and tell myself it's not happening, only it is. Somebody shouts through the letter-box. 'I know you're in there. Open this door'. So I do. And there is someone. It's a woman.

She said, 'Are you the son'? I said, 'What'? She said, 'Are you the son? I'm the daughter'. I said, 'Have you been watching the house'? She said, 'On and off. Why'? I said, 'Nothing'. She said, 'I don't know what there is to look so suited about'. I said, 'You'd better come in'.

*Go to black.*

*Come up on Graham as he puts a magazine on top of the wardrobe. He sits down in the easy chair. Night.*

It's nine o'clock when I hear the car outside. I'm sitting watching TV. I say, 'Oh hello. Did you have a nice time'? She said, 'Yes. Yes we did, thank you'. 'Did you get your sun tan lotion'? She said, 'What sun tan lotion'? 'You were going to get some sun tan lotion. Never mind. You've forgotten. How's Mr Turnbull'? 'Frank? He's all right'. She took her things off. 'I'm sure you could get to like him, Graham, if only you got to know him'. I said, 'Well, you should have brought him in'. 'Well, I will next time. It'd be nice if now and again we could go off as a threesome. What have you done'? 'Nothing', I said. 'Just sat here'. 'You've been all right'? 'Mmm'.

'You see', she said, 'there wasn't anybody outside'. 'Oh yes there was'. She said, 'Oh Graham. Have you had a tablet? Have a tablet'. 'I don't want a tablet. I'll tell you who was sat outside. Mrs Pamela Musgrave'. She said, 'Who's she'? 'Née Turnbull. The daughter of your hubby to be'. She said, 'He hasn't got a daughter. He's got a son down south. He hasn't got a daughter', she said, 'you're making stuff up now, have a tablet'. I said, 'I'm not making it up. And there's something else I'm not making up. Mrs Turnbull'. She said, 'There isn't a Mrs Turnbull. She's dead. I'm going to the lav'. I said, 'She's not dead. She's in a wheelchair with a broken heart. He's been having you on'.

After a bit she comes out. 'You're just saying all this'. 'The number's on the pad. Ring up. She's disabled is his wife. Has been for ten years. Their daughter looks after them. You're not the first. He's always doing it. One woman, it was going to be Barbados. Somebody spotted you together at Bolton Abbey. A well-wisher. Tenerife'!

Later on I took her a cup of tea. She'd been crying. She said, 'I bought this little bedjacket'. I said, 'I'm sorry, Mam'. She said, 'He was right enough. What can you expect at my age? How old am I'? 'Seventy-two'. 'That's another thing. I remembered with him. I don't remember with you'. I said, 'I'm sorry'. She said, 'You're not sorry. How are you sorry? You didn't like him'. I said, 'He wasn't good enough for you'. She said, 'I'm the best judge of that. He was natty, more than can be said for you'. And starts crying again. I said, 'I understand, Mam'. She said, 'You don't understand. How can you understand, you, you're not normal'? I said, 'I'm going to bed'.

In a bit she comes shouting outside the door. 'You think you've got it over me, Graham Whittaker. Well, you haven't. I've got it over you'. I said, 'Go back to bed'. She said, 'I know the kind of magazines you read'. I said, 'Chess. You'll catch cold'. She said, 'They never are chess. Chess with no clothes on. Chess in their birthday suits. That kind of chess. Chess men'. I said, 'Go to bed. And turn your blanket off'.

*Pause.*

Next day she's right as rain. Forgotten it. Never mentions it anyway, except just as we're coming out of the house she said, 'I do love you, Graham'. I said, 'I love you too'. She said, 'Anyway he had a hearing aid'. She said, 'What's on the agenda for today, then'? I said, 'I thought we might have a little ride to Ripon'. She said, 'Oh yes, Ripon. That's nice. We could go to the cathedral. We like old buildings, don't we, you and me'?

She put her arm through mine.

*Fade out.*

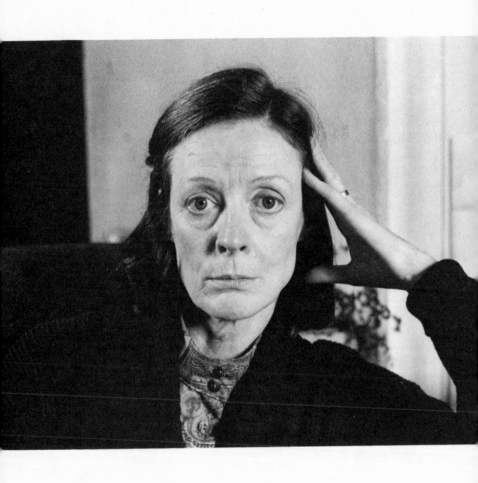

SUSAN: MAGGIE SMITH

# Bed Among the Lentils

*Susan is a vicar's wife. She is thin and nervous and probably smokes. She sits on an upright chair in the kitchen. It is evening.*

Geoffrey's bad enough but I'm glad I wasn't married to Jesus. The lesson this morning was the business in the Garden of Gethsemane when Jesus prays and the disciples keep falling asleep. He wakes them up and says, 'Could you not watch with me one hour'? It's my mother.

I overslept this morning, flung on a cardigan and got there just as everybody was standing up. It was Holy Communion so the militants were out in force, the sub-zero temperature in the side-chapel doubtless adding to the attraction.

Geoffrey kicks off by apologising for his failure to de-frost the church. (Subdued merriment.) Mr Medlicott has shingles, Geoffrey explains, and, as is well known, has consistently refused to initiate us lesser mortals into the mysteries of the boiler. (Helpless laughter.)

Mrs Belcher read the lesson. Mr Belcher took the plate round. 'Big day for you', I said to them afterwards.

The sermon was about sex. I didn't actually nod off, though I have heard it before. Marriage gives the OK to sex is the gist of it, but while it is far from being the be all and end all (you can say that again) sex is nevertheless the supreme joy of the married state and a symbol of the relationship between us and God. So, Geoffrey concludes, when we put our money in the plate it is a symbol of everything in our lives we are offering to God and that includes our sex. I could only find 10p.

Thinking about the sermon during the hymn I felt a pang of sympathy for the Deity, gifted with all this sex. No fun being made a present of the rare and desiccated conjunctions that take place between Geoffrey and me. Or the frightful collisions that presumably still occur between the Belchers. Not to mention whatever shamefaced fumblings go on between Miss Budd and Miss Bantock. 'It's all right if we offer it to God, Alice'. 'Well, if you say so, Pauline'.

Amazing scenes at the church door. Geoffrey had announced that after Easter the bishop would be paying us a visit so the fan club were running round in small circles, Miss Frobisher even going so far as to squeeze my elbow. Meanwhile, Geoffrey stands there the wind billowing out his surplice and ruffling his hair, what 'Who's Who in the Diocese of Ripon' calls 'his schoolboy good looks'. I helped put away the books while he did his 'underneath this cassock I am but a man like anybody else' act. 'Such a live wire', said Mrs Belcher, 'really putting the parish on the map'. 'That's right', burbles Mrs Shrubsole, looking at me. 'We must cherish him'.

We came back and I cherished him with some chicken wings in a tuna fish sauce. He said, 'That went down well'. I said, 'The chicken wings'? He said, 'My sermon. I felt it hit the nail on the head'. He put his hand over mine, hoping, I suppose, that having hit one nail he might hit another, but I said I had to go round with the parish magazine. 'Good girl', he said. 'I can attack my paperwork instead'.

Roads busy. Sunday afternoon. Families having a run out. Wheeling the pram, walking the dog. Living. Almighty God unto whom all hearts be open, and from whom no secrets are hid, cleanse the thoughts of our hearts by the inspiration of thy holy spirit that we may perfectly love thee and worthily magnify thy glorious name and not spend our Sunday afternoons parked in a lay-by on the Ring Road wondering what happened to our life.

When I got back Geoffrey was just off to Evensong, was I going to come? When I said 'No' he said, 'Really? Then I'd better pretend you have a headache'.

Why? One of the unsolved mysteries of life, or the unsolved mysteries of my life, is why the vicar's wife is expected to go to church at all. A barrister's wife doesn't have to go to court, an actor's wife isn't at every performance, so why have I always got to be on parade? Not to mention the larger question of whether one believes in God in the first place. It's assumed that being the vicar's wife one does but the question has never actually come up, not with Geoffrey anyway. I can understand why, of course. To look at me, the hair, the flat chest, the wan smile, you'd think I was just cut out for God. And maybe I am. I'd just like to have been asked that's all. Not that it matters of course. So long as you can run a tight jumble sale you can believe in what you like.

It could be that Geoffrey doesn't believe in God either. I've always longed to ask him only God never seems to crop up. 'Geoffrey', I'd say. 'Yes, Susan'? 'Do you really believe in God? I mean, cards on tables, you don't honestly, do you? God's just a job like any other. You've got to bring home the bacon somehow'. But no. Not a word. The subject's never discussed.

After he'd gone I discovered we were out of sherry so I've just been round to the off-licence. The woman served me. Didn't smile. I can't think why. I spend enough.

*Go to black.*

*Come up on Susan on the steps of the side-chapel, polishing a candlestick. Afternoon.*

We were discussing the ordination of women. The bishop asked me what I thought. Should women take the services? So long as it doesn't have to be me, I wanted to say, they can be taken by a trained gorilla. 'Oh yes', Geoffrey chips in, 'Susan's all in favour. She's keener than I am, aren't you, darling'? 'More sprouts anybody'? I said.

On the young side for a bishop, but he's been a prominent sportsman at university so that would explain it. Boxing or rugby. Broken nose at some stage anyway. One of the 'Christianity is common sense' brigade. Hobby's bricklaying apparently and refers to me throughout as 'Mrs Vicar'. Wants beer with his lunch and Geoffrey says he'll join him so this leaves me with the wine. Geoffrey's all over him because the rumour is he's shopping round for a new Archdeacon. Asks Geoff how outgoing I am. Actually says that. 'How outgoing is Mrs Vicar'? Mr Vicar jumps in with a quick rundown of my accomplishments and an outline of my punishing schedule. On a typical day, apparently, I kick off by changing the wheel on the Fiesta, then hasten to the bedside of a dying pensioner, after which, having done the altar flowers and dispensed warmth and appreciation to sundry parishioners en route, I top off a thrill-packed morning by taking round Meals on Wheels . . . somehow—'and this to me is the miracle', says Geoffrey—'somehow managing to rustle up a delicious lunch in the interim', the miracle somewhat belied by the flabby lasagna we are currently embarked on. 'The ladies', says the bishop. 'Where would we be without them'?

Disaster strikes as I'm doling out the tinned peaches: the jug into which I've decanted the Carnation milk gets knocked over, possibly by me. Geoffrey, for whom turning the other cheek is part of the job, claims it caught his elbow and his lordship takes the same line, insisting he gets doused in Carnation milk practically every day of his life. Still, when I get a dishcloth and sponge off his gaiters I catch him giving me a funny look. It's Mary Magdalen and the Nivea cream all over again. After lunch Geoffrey's supposed to be taking him on a tour of the parish but while we're having a cup of instant he claps his hand to his temple because he's suddenly remembered he's supposed to be in Keighley blessing a steam engine.

We're stacking the dishwasher and I ask Geoffrey how he thinks it's gone. Doesn't know. 'Fingers crossed', I say. 'I think there are more constructive things we could do than that', he says crisply, and goes off to mend his inner tube. I sit by the Aga for a bit and as I doze off it comes to me that by 'constructive things' he perhaps means prayer.

When I wake up there's a note from Geoffrey. 'Gone to talk to the Ladies Bright Hour. Go to bed'. I'm not sleepy and anyway we're running low on sherry so I drive into Leeds. I've stopped going round the corner now as I owe them a bit on the side and she's always so surly. There's a little Indian shop behind the Infirmary I've found. It's a newsagents basically but it sells drink and anything really, the way they do. Open last thing at night, Sundays included, my ideal. Ramesh he's called. Mr Ramesh I call him, though Ramesh may be his Christian name. Only not Christian of course. I've been once or twice now, only this time he sits me in the back place on a sack of something and talks. Little statuette of a god on the wall. A god. Not The God. Not the definite article. One of several thousand apparently. 'Safety in numbers', I said but he didn't understand. Looks a bit more fun than Jesus anyway. Shows me pictures of other gods, getting up to all sorts. I said, 'She looks a very busy lady. Is that yoga'? He said, 'Well, it helps'. He's quite athletic himself apparently, married, but his wife's only about fourteen so they won't let her in. He calls me Mrs Vicar too, only it's different. He has lovely teeth.

*Go to black.*

*Come up on Susan in the kitchen near the Aga. Morning.*

Once upon a time I had my life planned out . . . or half of it at any rate. I wasn't clear about the first part, but at the stroke of fifty I was all set to turn into a wonderful woman . . . the wife to a doctor, or a vicar's wife, Chairman of the Parish Council, a pillar of the WI. A wise, witty and ultimately white-haired old lady, who's always stood on her own feet until one day at the age of eighty she comes out of the County Library, falls under the weight of her improving book, breaks her hip and dies peacefully, continently and without fuss under a snowy coverlet in the cottage hospital. And coming away from her funeral in a country churchyard on a bright winter's afternoon people would say, 'Well, she was a wonderful woman'.

Had this been a serious ambition I should have seen to it I was equipped with the skills necessary to its achievement. How to produce jam which, after reaching a good, rolling boil, successfully coats the spoon; how to whip up a Victoria sponge that just gives to the fingertips; how to plan, execute and carry through a successful garden fête. All weapons in the armoury of any upstanding Anglican lady. But I can do none of these things. I'm even a fool at the flower arrangement. I ought to have a PhD in the subject the number of classes I've been to but still my efforts show as much evidence of art as walking sticks in an umbrella stand. Actually it's temperament. I don't have it. If you think squash is a competitive activity try flower arrangement.

On this particular morning the rota has Miss Frobisher and Mrs Belcher down for the side aisles and I'm paired with Mrs Shrubsole to do the altar and the lectern. My honest opinion, never voiced needless to say, is that if they were really sincere about religion they'd forget flower arrangement altogether, invest in some permanent plastic jobs and put the money towards the current most popular famine. However, around mid-morning I wander over to the church with a few dog-eared chrysanthemums. They look as if they could do with an immediate drink so I call in at the vestry and root out a vase or two from the cupboard where Geoffrey keeps the communion wine.

It not looming very large on my horizon, I assume I am doing the altar and Mrs Shrubsole the lectern, but when I come out of the vestry Mrs S is at the altar well embarked on her arrangement. I said, 'I thought I was doing the altar'. She said, 'No. I think Mrs Belcher will bear me out. I'm down to do the altar. You are doing the lectern. Why'? She smiled sweetly. 'Do you have a preference'? The only preference I have is to shove my chrysanthemums up her nose but instead I practise a bit of Christian forbearance and go stick them in a vase by the lectern. In the best tradition of my floral arrangements they look like the poles of a wigwam, so I go and see if I can cadge a bit of backing from Mrs Belcher. 'Are you using this'? I say, picking up a bit of mouldy old fern. 'I certainly am. I need every bit of my spiraea. It gives it body'. I go over and see if Miss Frobisher has any greenery going begging only she's doing some Japanese number, a vase like a test-tube half filled with gravel, in which she's throttling a lone carnation. So I retire to the vestry for a bit to calm my shattered nerves, and when I come out ready to tackle my chrysanths again Mrs Shrubsole has apparently finished and fetched the other two up to the altar to admire her handiwork. So I wander up and take a look.

Well, it's a brown job, beech leaves, teazles, grass, that school of thought. Mrs Shrubsole is saying, 'It's called Forest Murmurs. It's what I did for my Highly Commended at Harrogate last year. What do you think'? Gert and Daisy are of course speechless with admiration, but when I tentatively suggest it might look a bit better if she cleared up all the bits and pieces lying around she said, 'What bits and pieces'? I said, 'All these acorns and fir-cones and what not. What's this conker in aid of'? She said, 'Leave that. The whole arrangement pivots on that'. I said, 'Pivots'? 'When the adjudicator was commenting on my arrangement he particularly singled out the hint I gave of the forest floor'. I said, 'Mrs Shrubsole. This is the altar of St Michael and All Angels. It is not The Wind in the Willows'. Mrs Belcher said, 'I think you ought to sit down'. I said, 'I do not want to sit down'. I said, 'It's all very well to transform the altar into something out of Bambi but do not forget that for the vicar the altar is his working surface. Furthermore', I added, 'should the vicar sink to his knees in prayer, which since this is the altar he is wont to do, he is quite likely to get one of these teazle things in his eye. This is not a flower arrangement. It is a booby trap. A health hazard. In fact', I say in a moment of supreme inspiration, 'it should be labelled HAZFLOR. Permit me to demonstrate'. And I begin getting down on my knees just to prove how lethal her bloody Forest Murmurs is. Only I must have slipped because next thing I know I'm rolling down the altar steps and end up banging my head on the communion rail.

Mrs Shrubsole, who along with every other organisation known to man has been in the St John's Ambulance Brigade, wants me left lying down, whereas Mrs Belcher is all for getting me on to a chair. 'Leave them lying down', says Mrs Belcher, 'and they inhale their own vomit. It happens all the time, Veronica'. 'Only, Muriel', says Mrs Shrubsole, 'when they have vomited. She hasn't vomited'. 'No',

I say, 'but I will if I have to listen to any more of this drivel', and begin to get up. 'Is that blood, Veronica'? says Mrs Belcher pointing to my head. 'Well', says Mrs Shrubsole, reluctant to concede to Mrs B on any matter remotely touching medicine, 'it could be, I suppose. What we need is some hot sweet tea'. 'I thought that theory had been discredited', says Mrs Belcher. Discredited or not it sends Miss Frobisher streaking off to find a teabag, and also, it subsequently transpires, to telephone all and sundry in an effort to locate Geoffrey. He is in York taking part in the usual interdenominational conference on the role of the church in a hitherto uncolonised department of life, underfloor central heating possibly. He comes haring back thinking I'm at death's door, and finding I'm not has nothing more constructive to offer than I take a nap.

This gives the fan club the green light to invade the vicarage, making endless tea and the vicar his lunch and, as he puts it, 'spoiling him rotten'. Since this also licenses them to conduct a fact-finding survey of all the housekeeping arrangements or absence of same ('Where does she keep the Duroglit, vicar'?), a good time is had by all. Meanwhile Emily Brontë is laid out on the sofa in a light doze.

I come round to hear Geoffrey saying, 'Mrs Shrubsole's going now, darling'. I don't get up. I never even open my eyes. I just wave and say, 'Goodbye, Mrs Shrubsole'. Only thinking about it as I drift off again I think I may have said, 'Goodbye, Mrs Subsoil'. Anyway I meant the other. Shrubsoil.

When I woke up it was dark and Geoffrey'd gone out. I couldn't find a thing in the cupboard so I got the car out and drove into Leeds. I sat in the shop for a bit, not saying much. Then I felt a bit wanny and Mr Ramesh let me go into the back place to lie down. I must have dozed off because when I woke up Mr Ramesh has come in and started taking off his clothes. I said, 'What are you doing? What about the shop'? He said, 'Do not worry about the shop. I have closed the shop'. I said, 'It's only nine. You don't close till eleven'. 'I do tonight', he said. I said, 'What's tonight'? He said, 'A chance in a million. A turn-up for the books. Will you take your clothes off please'. And I did.

*Go to black.*

*Come up on Susan sitting in the vestry having a cigarette. Afternoon.*

You never see pictures of Jesus smiling, do you? I mentioned this to Geoffrey once. 'Good point, Susan', is what he said, which made me wish I'd not brought it up in the first place. Said I should think of Our Lord as having an inward smile, the doctrine according to Geoffrey being that Jesus was made man so he smiled, laughed and did everything else just like the rest of us. 'Do you think he ever smirked'? I asked, whereupon Geoffrey suddenly remembered he was burying somebody in five minutes and took himself off.

If Jesus *is* all man I just wish they'd put a bit more of it into the illustrations. I was sitting in church yesterday, wrestling with this point of theology, when it occurred to me that something seemed to have happened to Geoffrey. The service should have kicked off ages ago but he's still in the vestry. Mr Bland is filling in with something uplifting on the organ and Miss Frobisher, never one to let an opportunity slip, has slumped to her knees for a spot of unscheduled silent prayer. Mrs Shrubsole is lost in contemplation of the altar, still adorned with Forest Murmurs, a trail of ivy round the cross the final inspired touch. Mr Bland now ups the volume but still no sign of Geoff. 'Arnold', says Mrs Belcher, 'there seems to be some hiatus in the proceedings', and suddenly the fan club is on red alert. She's just levering him to his feet when I get in first and nip into the vestry to investigate.

His reverence is there, white-faced, every cupboard open and practically in tears. He said, 'Have you seen it'? I said, 'What'? He said, 'The wine. The communion wine. It's gone'. I said, 'That's no tragedy', and offer to pop out and get some ordinary. Geoffrey said, 'They're not open. Besides, what does it look like'? I said, 'Well, it looks like we've run out of communion wine'. He said, 'We haven't run out. There was a full bottle here on Friday. Somebody has drunk it'.

It's on the tip of my tongue to say that if Jesus is all he's cracked up to be why doesn't he use tap-water and put it to the test when I suddenly remember that Mr Bland keeps a bottle of cough mixture in his cupboard in case any of the choirboys gets chesty. At the thought of celebrating the Lord's Supper in Benylin Geoffrey now has a complete nervous breakdown but, as I point out, it's red and sweet and nobody is going to notice. Nor do they. I see Mr Belcher licking his lips a bit thoughtfully as he walks back down the aisle but that's all. 'What was the delay'? asks Mrs Shrubsole. 'Nothing', I said, 'just a little hiccup'.

Having got it right for once I'm feeling quite pleased with myself, but Geoffrey obviously isn't and never speaks all afternoon so I bunk off Evensong and go into Leeds.

Mr Ramesh has evidently been expecting me because there's a bed made up in the storeroom upstairs. I go up first and get in. When I'm in bed I can put my hand out and feel the lentils running through my fingers. When he comes up he's put on his proper clothes. Long white shirt, sash and what not. Loincloth underneath. All spotless. Like Jesus. Only not. I watch him undress and think about them all at Evensong and Geoffrey praying in that pausy way he does, giving you time to mean each phrase. And the fan club lapping it up, thinking they love God when they just love Geoffrey. Lighten our darkness we beseech thee O Lord and by thy great mercy defend us from all perils and dangers of this night. Like Mr Ramesh who is twenty-six with lovely legs, who goes swimming every morning at Merrion Street Baths and plays hockey for Horsforth. I ask him if they offer their sex to God. He isn't very interested in the point but with them, so far as I can gather, sex is all part of God anyway. I can see why too. It's the first time I really understand what all the fuss is about. There among the lentils on the second Sunday after Trinity.

I've just popped into the vestry. He's put a lock on the cupboard door.

*Go to black.*

*Come up on Susan sitting in the drawing-room of the vicarage. Much smarter than in previous scenes, she has had her hair done and seems a different woman. Evening.*

I stand up and say, 'My name is Susan. I am a vicar's wife and I am an alcoholic'. Then I tell my story. Or some of it anyway. 'Don't pull any punches', says Clem, my counsellor. 'Nobody's going to be shocked, believe me, love, we've all been there'. But I don't tell them about Mr Ramesh because they've not been there. 'Listen, people. I was so drunk I used to go and sleep with an Asian grocer. Yes, and you won't believe this. I loved it. Loved every minute'. Dear oh dear. This was a real drunken lady.

So I draw a veil over Mr Ramesh who once, on the feast of St Simon and St Jude (Choral Evensong at six, daily services at the customary hour), put make-up on his eyes and bells on his ankles, and naked except for his little belt danced in the back room of the shop with a tambourine.

'So how did you come to AA'? they ask. 'My husband', I say. 'The vicar. He persuaded me'. But I lie. It was not my husband, it was Mr Ramesh, the exquisitely delicate and polite Mr Ramesh who one Sunday night turned his troubled face towards me with its struggling moustache and asked if he might take the bull by the horns and enquire if intoxication was a prerequisite for sexual intercourse, or whether it was only when I was going to bed with him, the beautiful Mr Ramesh, twenty-six, with wonderful legs, whether it was only with him I had to be inebriated. And was it, asked this slim, flawless and troubled creature, was it perhaps his colour? Because if not he would like to float the suggestion that sober might be even nicer. So the credit for the road to Damascus goes to Mr Ramesh, whose first name turns out also to be Ramesh. Ramesh Ramesh, a member of the community council and the Leeds Federation of Trade.

But none of this I say. In fact I never say anything at all. Only when it becomes plain to Geoffrey (and it takes all of three weeks) that Mrs Vicar is finally on the wagon, who is it gets the credit? Not one of Mr Ramesh's jolly little gods, busy doing everything under the sun to one another, much like Mr Ramesh. Oh no. It's full marks to Geoffrey's chum, the Deity, moving in his well-known mysterious way.

So now everything has changed. For the moment I am a new woman and Geoffrey is a new man. And he brings it up on the slightest pretext. 'My wife's an alcoholic, you know. Yes. It's a great challenge to me and to the parish as extended family'. From being a fly in the ointment I find myself transformed into a feather in his cap. Included it in his sermon on Prayers Answered when he reveals that he and the fan club have been having these jolly get togethers in which they'd all prayed over what he calls 'my problem'. It practically sent me racing back to the Tio Pepe even to think of it. The fans, of course, never dreaming that their prayers would be answered, are furious. They think it's brought us closer together. Geoffrey thinks that too. We were at some doleful diocesan jamboree last week and I'm stuck there clutching my grapefruit juice as Geoffrey's telling the tale to some bearded cleric. Suddenly he seizes my hand. 'We met it with love', he cries, as if love were some all-purpose antibiotic, which to Geoffrey it probably is.

And it goes on, the mileage in it endless. I said to Geoffrey that when I stood up at AA I sometimes told the story about the flower arranging. Result: he starts telling it all over the diocese. The first time was at a conference on The Supportive Parish. Gales of deep, liberated, caring laughter. He's now given it a new twist and tells the story as if he's talking about a parishioner, then at the end he says, 'Friends I want to tell you something. (Deep hush.) That drunken flower-arranger was my wife'. Silence . . . then the applause, *terrific*.

I've caught the other young, upwardly mobile parsons sneaking looks at me now and again and you can see them thinking why weren't they smart enough to marry an alcoholic or better still a drug addict, problem wives whom they could do a nice redemption job on, right there on their own doorstep. Because there's no stopping Geoffrey now. He grips my hand in public, nay *brandishes* it. 'We're a team', he cries. Looks certain to be rural dean and that's only the beginning. As the bishop says, 'Just the kind of man we're looking for on the bench . . . someone with a seasoned compassion, someone who's looked life in the face. Someone who's been there'.

Mr Ramesh sold his shop. He's gone back to India to fetch his wife. She's old enough now apparently. I went down there on Sunday. There was a boy writing Under New Management on the window. Spelled wrong. And something underneath in Hindi, spelled right probably. He said he thought Mr Ramesh would be getting another shop, only in Preston.

They do that, of course, Asians, build something up, get it going nicely, then take the profit and move on. It's a good thing. We ought to be more like that, more enterprising.

My group meets twice a week and I go. Religiously. And that's what it is, of course. The names are different, Frankie and Steve, Susie and Clem. But it's actually Miss Frobisher and Mrs Shrubsole all over again. I never liked going to one church so I end up going to two. Geoffrey would call that the wonderful mystery of God. I call it bad taste. And I wouldn't do it to a dog. But that's the thing nobody ever says about God . . . he has no taste at all.

*Fade out.*

IRENE RUDDOCK: PATRICIA ROUTLEDGE

# A Lady of Letters

*Miss Ruddock is an ordinary middle-aged woman. The room in which we see her is simply furnished and there is a bay window. It is afternoon.*

I can't say the service was up to scratch. It smacked of the conveyor-belt. In fact I wrote to the crematorium. I said I thought the hallmark of a ceremony of that nature was reverence, whereas the word that kept coming into my mind was brisk. Moreover, I added, grief-stricken people do not expect to emerge from the Chapel of Rest to find grown men skulking in the rhododendrons with tab-ends in their mouths. If the hearse drivers must smoke then facilities should be provided. I'd heard good reports of this crematorium, but I hoped that they would agree with me that on this occasion it had let itself down.

Of course if I'd happened to be heartbroken I'd have felt much worse. I didn't let on to the crematorium because I thought it might get them off the hook but I actually didn't know her all that well. I used to see her getting on the 37 and we'd pass the time of day. She lost her mother round about the time I lost mine, she had a niece in Australia and I have the one cousin in Canada, then she went in for gas-fired central heating just a few weeks before I did, so one way and another we covered a lot of the same ground. I'd spent years thinking she was called Hammersley, which was way off the mark because her name turns out to be Pringle. There was a picture of her in the *Evening Post* (she'd been a big voluntary worker) with details of the funeral on the Wednesday afternoon, which is the one time I'm dangling my feet a bit, so I thought I'd get out my little maroon coat and put in an appearance. At least it's an outing. And I was glad I'd gone but, as I say, the ceremony was a bit lack-lustre and topped off by these young fellers smoking, so I thought the least I could do was write.

Anyway I had a charming letter back from the director of operations, a Mr Widdop. He said he was most grateful I'd drawn this matter to his attention and, while he was aware the practice sometimes went on, if he personally caught anybody smoking he would jump on the culprits with both feet. He knew I would appreciate that discipline within the chapel precincts presented special problems as it wasn't always convenient to tear a strip off somebody when there were grief-stricken people knocking about. What he personally preferred to do was to keep a low profile, then come down on the offenders like a ton of bricks once the coast was clear. With regard to my remarks about facilities, they had no plans to provide a smoking area in the Chapel of Rest in the foreseeable future as I must understand that space was at a premium and top of their list of priorities at the present moment was the provision of a temporary temple for the use of racial minorities. However, he would bear my remarks in mind, and if I were to come across any similar infringements in the future I was not to hesitate to get in touch.

I wrote him a little letter back thanking him for his prompt and courteous reply and saying that though I hoped not to be making any further visits to the crematorium in the near future (joke) I took his point. I also dropped a line to the relatives, care of the undertakers, saying that I was an acquaintance of Miss Pringle, had been present at the ceremony and had taken the liberty of entering into correspondence with the crematorium over the unfortunate lapse. I enclosed a copy of Mr Widdop's reply but they didn't write back, which I can understand because the one thing death always entails is a mass of correspondence. When Mother died I had fifty-three letters. Besides, they may not have even seen them smoking, they were probably blinded with grief. I see we've got a new couple moved in opposite. Don't look very promising. The kiddy looks filthy.

*Go to black.*

*Come up on Miss Ruddock in the same setting. Morning.*

A card from the opticians this morning saying that their records indicate that it's two years since they supplied me with spectacles and that by now they would almost certainly be in need of verification and suggesting I call at my earliest convenience. I thought that was nice so I took my trusty Platignum and dashed off an answer forthwith. I said I thought it was very considerate of them to have kept me in mind and while I was quite satisfied with my spectacles at the present moment I was grateful to them for drawing the matter to my attention and in the event of my noticing any deterioration I would in due course get in touch with them. (*She picks up her pen.*) It's stood me in good stead has this pen. Mother bought it me the last time she was able to get over to Harrogate. It's been a real friend. (*She glances in the direction of the window.*)

Angie her name is. I heard him shout of her as I went by en route for the Post Office. He was laid out underneath his car wanting a spanner and she came out, transistor in one hand, kiddy in the other. Thin little thing, bruise on its arm. I thought, 'Well, you've got a car, you've got a transistor, it's about time you invested in some curtains'. She can't be more than twenty and by the look of her she's expecting another.

I passed the place where there was the broken step I wrote to the council was a danger to the public. Little ramp there now, access for the disabled. Whenever I pass I think, 'Well, that's thanks to you, Irene'. My monument that ramp. Only some dog had gone and done its business right in the middle of it. I'm sure there's more of that than there used to be. I had a little Awayday to London last year and it was dog dirt everywhere. I spotted some on the pavement right outside Buckingham Palace. I wrote to the Queen about it. Had a charming letter back from a lady in waiting saying that Her Majesty appreciated my interest and that my letter had been passed on to the appropriate authority. The upshot eventually is I get a long letter from the chief cleansing officer to Westminster City Council apologising profusely and enclosing a rundown of their Highways and Maintenance Budget. That's been my experience generally . . . people are only too grateful to have these things pointed out. The keynote is participation. Of course I wrote back to thank him and then blow me if I didn't get another letter thanking me for mine. So I wrote back saying I hadn't been expecting another letter and there was no need to have written again and was this an appropriate use of public resources? They didn't even bother to reply. Typical.

*Pause.*

I'm just waiting for the paper coming. Not that there's much in it. The correspondence I initiated on the length of the Archbishop of Canterbury's hair seems to have gone off the boil. Till I wrote up to Live Letters nobody'd actually spotted it. Various people took up the

cudgels until there was an impassioned letter from the Rural Dean of Halifax who has a beard and that seems to have put the tin hat on it.
Getting dark.
The couple opposite just having their tea. No cloth on. They must have put the kiddy to bed. When I put the milk bottle out I heard it crying.

*Go to black.*

*Come up on Miss Ruddock sitting in an easy chair reading the newspaper. Afternoon.*

Prison, they have it easy. Television, table tennis, art. It's just a holiday camp, do you wonder there's crime? And people say, 'Well, what can you do'? Well, you can get on to your MP for a start. I do, regularly. Got a reply to one letter this morning. I'd written drawing his attention to a hitherto unnoticed factor in the rise in crime, namely the number of policemen these days who wear glasses. What chance would they have against a determined assailant? He noted my comments and promised to make them known in the proper quarter. He's Labour but it's always very good notepaper and beautifully typed.

When I'd dusted round and done my jobs I had a walk on to the end and bought a little packet of pork sausage and some Basildon Bond. Big black hair in the sausage. So I wrote off to the makers enclosing the hair. Stuck it under a bit of sellotape. Little arrow: 'This is the hair'. I emphasised that I didn't want a substitute packet, as it was plainly manufactured under unhygienic conditions, so would they send me a refund of the purchase price plus the cost of postage. I don't want inundating with sausage.

I keep wondering about the kiddy opposite. Haven't seen it for a week or two. And they're out all the time. Every single night they go off, and the kiddy doesn't go. And nobody comes in to sit. It can't be more than five. Where do they get the money to go out, that's what I'd like to know? Because he's not working. Spends all day tinkering with that car. There wants to be a bit less of the car and a bit more of the kiddy. It never plays out and they want fresh air do kiddies, it's a well-known fact. You don't hear it crying now, nothing. And I've never seen a cloth on. Teapot stuck there. Milk bottle. It'll surprise me if they're married. He has a tattoo anyway.

*Go to black.*

*Come up on Miss Ruddock sitting on a dining chair in the*
*window. Dusk.*

My mother knew everybody in this street. She could reel off the
occupants of every single house. Everybody could, once upon a time.
Now, they come and they go. That's why these tragedies happen.
Nobody watching. If they knew they were being watched they might
behave. I'd talk to next door's about it only there hasn't been any
contact since the business over the dustbins. And this other side's
Asians so they won't know what's normal and what isn't. Though I've
a feeling he's been educated and their kiddies are always beautifully
turned out. I just wish they'd do something about their privet.

I thought I'd go and have a word with the doctor, drop a hint there
somehow. There used to be just one doctor. Now they've all
amalgamated so it's a bit of a lucky dip. Young fellow. I said I was
getting upset, like I did before. 'Before what'? he said. I said, 'It's in
my notes'. So he read them and then said, 'You've been getting a bit
upset, like you did before. I'll give you something to take'. So I told
him about the kiddy, and he said, 'Well, these tablets will help you to
take a more balanced view'. I gave them three or four days and they
didn't seem to me to make much difference so I went along again.
Different doctor this time. Same rigmarole. I said I didn't want any
more tablets, I just wanted the name of the firm manufacturing the
ones I'd already had, because I think they ought to be told if their
product isn't doing the trick. The doctor said it would be easier if he
gave me some new tablets and anyway I couldn't write, the firm was
Swiss. I said, 'What difference does that make, everybody speaks
English now'. He said, 'We don't want to get into that, do we'? and
writes me another prescription. I shan't bother with it. In fact I put it
down the toilet. I don't know who you write to about doctors.

After I'd had my tea I sat in the front room in the dark watching the
house. He's messing about with the car, one of those little vests on
they have now without sleeves. Radio going hammer and tongs. No
kiddy still. I don't even know their name.

*Go to black.*

*Come up on Miss Ruddock in her hat and coat against a*
*bare background.*

Thinking about it afterwards, I realised it must have been the doctor that alerted the vicar. Came round anyway. Not the old vicar. I'd have known him. This was a young fellow in a collar and tie, could have been anybody. I didn't take the chain off. I said, 'How do I know you're the vicar, have you any identification'? He shoves a little cross round the door. I said, 'What's this'? He said, 'A cross'. I said, 'A cross doesn't mean anything. Youths wear crosses nowadays. Hooligans. They wear crosses in their ears'. He said, 'Not like this. This is a real cross. A working cross. It's the tool of my trade'. I was still a bit dubious, then I saw he had cycle clips on so I let him in.

He chats for a bit, this and that, no mention of God for long enough. They keep him up their sleeve for as long as they can, vicars, they know it puts people off. Went through a long rigmarole about love. How love comes in different forms . . . loving friends, loving the countryside, loving music. People would be surprised to learn, he said (and I thought, 'Here we go'), people would be surprised to learn that they loved God all the time and just didn't know it. I cut him short. I said, 'If you've come round here to talk about God you're barking up the wrong tree. I'm an atheist'. He was a bit stumped, I could see. They don't expect you to be an atheist when you're a miss. Vicars, they think if you're a single person they're on a good wicket. He said, 'Well, Miss Ruddock, I shall call again. I shall look on you as a challenge'.

He hadn't been gone long when there's another knock, only this time it's a policeman, with a woman policeman in tow. Ask if they can come in and have a word. I said, 'What for'? He said, 'You know what for'. I said, 'I don't', but I let them in. Takes his helmet off, only young and says he'll come straight to the point: was it me who'd been writing these letters? I said, 'What letters? I don't write letters'. He said, 'Letters'. I said, 'Everyone writes letters. I bet you write letters'. He said, 'Not like you, love'. I said, 'Don't love me. You'd better give me your name and number. I intend to write to your superintendent'.

It turns out it's to do with the couple opposite. I said, 'Well, why are you asking me'? He said, 'We're asking you because who was it wrote to the chemist saying his wife was a prostitute? We're asking you because who was it gave the lollipop man a nervous breakdown'? I said, 'Well, he was interfering with those children'. He said, 'The court bound you over to keep the peace. This is a serious matter'. I said, 'It is a serious matter. I can't keep the peace when there's cruelty and neglect going on under my nose. I shouldn't keep the peace when there's a child suffering. It's not my duty to keep the peace then, is it'? So then madam takes over, the understanding approach. She said didn't I appreciate this was a caring young couple? I said if they were a caring young couple why did you never see the kiddy? If they were a caring young couple why did they go gadding off every night, leaving the kiddy alone in the house? She said because the kiddy wasn't alone in the house. The kiddy wasn't in the house. The kiddy was in hospital in Bradford, that's where they were going every night. And that's where the kiddy died, last Friday. I said, 'What of? Neglect'? She said, 'No. Leukaemia'.

*Pause.*

He said, 'You'd better get your hat and coat on'.

*Go to black.*

*Come up on Miss Ruddock back at home. Day.*

I've got two social workers come, one white, one black. Maureen I'm supposed to call the white one, shocking finger nails, ginger hair, and last week a hole in her tights as big as a 50p piece. She looks more in need of social work than I do. Puts it all down to men. 'We all know about men, don't we, Irene'. I never said she could call me Irene. I don't want to be called Irene. I want to be called Miss Ruddock. I'm not Irene. I haven't been Irene since Mother died. But they all call me Irene, her, the police, everybody. They think they're being nice, only it's just a nice way of being nasty. The other one's Asian, Mrs Rabindi, little red spot on her forehead, all that. Sits, talks. She's right enough. Said I'd be useful in India. You can earn a living writing letters there apparently as they're all illiterate. Something daubed on her door last week. She says it's what you get to expect if you're Asian. I said, 'Well, there's all sorts gets chucked over my wall'. We sit and talk, only she's a bit of a boring woman. I tell her I loved my mother and she says how she loved her mother. I tell her I'm frightened to walk the streets and she tells me how she's been attacked herself. Well, it doesn't get you any further. It's all 'me too'. Social work, I think it's just chiming in.

I'm on what's called a suspended sentence. It means you have to toe the line. If I write any more letters I get sent to prison. The magistrate said I was more to be pitied than anything else. I said, 'Excuse me, could I interject'? He said, 'No. Your best plan would be to keep mum'. Big fellow, navy blue suit, poppy in his buttonhole. Looked a bit of a drinker.

Maureen says I should listen to local radio. Join these phone-in things. Chat to the disc jockey and choose a record. She says they're very effective in alleviating loneliness and a sense of being isolated in the community. I said, 'Yes and they're even more effective in bumping up the phone bill'. Maureen's trying to get me on reading. I suppose to get me off writing. She says books would widen my horizon. Fetches me novels, but they don't ring true. I mean, when somebody in a novel says something like 'I've never been in an air crash', you know this means that five minutes later they will be. Say trains never crash and one does. In stories saying it brings it on. So if you get the heroine saying, 'I don't suppose I shall ever be happy', then you can bank on it there's happiness just around the corner. That's the rule in novels. Whereas in life you can say you're never going to be happy and you never are happy, and saying it doesn't make a ha'porth of difference. That's the real rule. Sometimes I catch myself thinking it'll be better the second time round. (*Pause.*) But this is it. This has been my go.

*Pause.*

New policeman now. Walks the streets, the way they used to. Part of the new policy. Community policing. Smiles. Passes the time of day. Keeping an eye on things.

Certainly keeps an eye on No. 56. In there an hour at a stretch. Timed it the other day and when eventually he comes out she's at the door in just a little shorty housecoat thing.

He's in there now.

*Pause.*

He wants reporting.

*Go to black.*

*Come up on Miss Ruddock against a plain institutional*
*background. She is in a tracksuit, speaks very quickly and*
*is radiant.*

I ought to be writing up my diary. Mrs Proctor's got us all on
keeping diaries as part of Literary Appreciation. The other girls can't
think what to put in theirs, me I can't think what to leave out.
Trouble is I never have time to write it up, I'm three days behind as it
is.

I'm that busy. In a morning it's Occupation and I've opted for
bookbinding and dressmaking. In dressmaking Mrs Dunlop's
chucked me in at the deep end and I'm running up a little cocktail
dress. I said, 'I never have cocktails'. She said, 'Well, now you've got
the dress, you can'. That's what it's geared to, this place, new
horizons. It's in shantung with a little shawl collar. Lucille's making
me a chunky necklace for it in Handicrafts.

I share a room with Bridget, who's from Glasgow. She's been a
prostitute on and off and did away with her kiddy, accidentally, when
she was drunk and upset. Bonny little face, you'd never think it. Her
mother was blind, but made beautiful pastry and brought up a family
of nine in three rooms. You don't know you're born I think. I'm
friends with practically everyone though besides Bridget. I'm up and
down this corridor; more often than not I'm still on my rounds when
the bell goes.

They laugh at me, I know, but it's all in good part. Lucille says,
'You're funny you, Irene. You don't mind being in prison'. I said,
'Prison'! I said, 'Lucille. This is the first taste of freedom I've had in
years'.

Of course I'm lucky. The others miss the sex. Men, men, men.
They talk about nothing else.

Mind you, that's not quite the closed book it used to be. Bridget's
taken me through the procedure step by step and whereas previous to
this if I'd ever found myself in bed with a man I should have been like
a fish out of water, now, as Bridget says, at least I know the rudiments.
Of course I can't ever see it coming to that at my age, but still it's nice
to have another string to your bow. They've got me smoking now and
again as well. I mean, I shan't ever be a full-time smoker, I'm not that
type, and I don't want to be, but it means that if I'm ever in a social
situation when I'm called on to smoke, like when they're toasting the

Queen, I shan't be put off my stroke. But you see, that's the whole philosophy of this place: acquiring skills.

I sailed through the secretarial course, Miss Macaulay says I'm their first Grade I. I can type like the wind. Miss Macaulay says we mustn't let the grass grow under our feet and if she goes down on her knees in Admin they might (repeat might) let me have a go on their word processor. Then the plan is: Stage One, I go on day release for a bit, followed by Stage Two a spell in a resettlement hostel where I'll be reintegrated into the community. Then finally Stage Three a little job in an office somewhere. I said to Miss Macaulay, 'Will it matter my having been in prison'? She said, 'Irene, with your qualifications it wouldn't matter if you'd been in the SS'.

But the stuff some of them come out with! You have to smile. They have words for things I didn't know there were words for, and in fact I swear myself on occasion now, though only when the need arises. The other evening I'm sat with Shirley during Association. Shirley's very obese, I think it's glandular, and we're trying to put together a letter to her boy friend. Well, she says it's her boy friend only I had to start the letter three times because first go off she says his name's Kenneth, then she says it's Mark, and finally she settles on Stephen. She stammers does Shirley and I think she just wanted a name she could say. I don't believe she has a boy friend at all, just wants to be in the swim. She shouldn't actually be in here in fact, she's not all there but there's nowhere else to put her apparently, she sets fire to places. Anyway, we're sitting in her room concocting this letter to her pretend boy friend when Black Geraldine waltzes in and drapes herself across the bed and starts chipping in, saying was this boy friend blond, did he have curly hair, and then nasty personal-type questions she should know better than to ask Shirley. And Shirley's getting confused and stammering and Geraldine's laughing, so finally I threw caution to the winds and told Geraldine to fuck up.

She screams with laughing and goes running down the corridor saying, 'Do you know what Irene said, do you know what Irene said'? When she'd gone Shirley said, 'You shouldn't have said that'. I said, 'I know, but sometimes it's necessary'. She said, 'No, Irene. I don't mean you shouldn't have said it. Only you got it wrong. It's not fuck up'. I said, 'What is it'? She said, 'It's fuck off'. She's good-hearted.

*Pause.*

Sometimes Bridget will wake up in the middle of the night shouting, dreaming about the kiddy she killed, and I go over and sit by the bed and hold her hand till she's gone off again. There's my little clock ticking and I can hear the wind in the poplar trees by the playing field and maybe it's raining and I'm sitting there. And I'm so *happy.*

*Fade out.*

LESLEY: JULIE WALTERS

# Her Big Chance

*Lesley is in her early thirties. She is in her flat. Morning.*

I shot a man last week. In the back. I miss it now, it was really interesting. Still, I'm not going to get depressed about it. You have to look to the future. To have something like that under your belt can be quite useful, you never know when you might be called on to repeat the experience.

It wasn't in the line of duty. I wasn't a policewoman or someone who takes violence in their stride. It was with a harpoon gun actually, but it definitely wasn't an accident. My decision to kill was arrived at only after a visible tussle with my conscience. I had to make it plain that once I'd pulled the trigger things were never going to be the same again: this was a woman at the crossroads.

It wasn't Crossroads, of course. They don't shoot people in Crossroads, at any rate not with harpoon guns. If anybody did get shot it would be with a weapon more suited to the motel ambience. I have been in Crossroads though, actually. I was in an episode involving a fork lunch. At least I was told it was a fork lunch, the script said it was a finger buffet. I said to the floor manager, I said, 'Rex. Are you on cans because I'd like some direction on this point. Are we toying or are we tucking in'? He said, 'Forget it. We're losing the food anyway'. I was playing Woman in a Musquash Coat, a guest at a wedding reception, and I was scheduled just to be in that one episode. However in my performance I tried to suggest I'd taken a fancy to the hotel in the hope I might catch the director's eye and he'd have me stay on after the fork lunch for the following episode which involved a full-blown weekend. So I acted an interest in the soft furnishings, running my fingers over the formica and admiring the carpet on the walls. Only Rex came over to say that they'd put me in a musquash coat to suggest I was a sophisticated woman, could I try and look as if I was more at home in a three star motel. I wasn't at home in that sort of motel I can tell you. I said to the man I'd been put next to, who I took to be my husband, I said, 'Curtains in orange nylon and no place mats, there's not even the veneer of civilisation'. He said, 'Don't talk to me about orange nylon. I was on a jury once that sentenced Richard Attenborough to death'. We'd been told to indulge in simulated cocktail chit-chat so we weren't being unprofessional, talking. That is something I pride myself on, actually: I am professional to my fingertips.

Whatever it is I'm doing, even if it's just a walk-on, I must must must get involved, right up to the hilt. I can't help it. People who know me tell me I'm a very serious person, only it's funny, I never get to do serious parts. The parts I get offered tend to be fun-loving girls who take life as it comes and aren't afraid of a good time should the opportunity arise-type-thing. I'd call them vivacious if that didn't carry overtones of the outdoor life. In a nutshell I play the kind of girl who's very much at home on a bar stool and who seldom has to light her own cigarette. That couldn't be more different from me because for a start I'm not a smoker. I mean, I can smoke if a part requires it. I'm a professional and you need as many strings to your bow as you can in this game. But, having said that, I'm not a natural smoker and what's more I surprise my friends by not being much of a party-goer either. (Rather curl up with a book quite frankly.) *However*, this particular party I'd made an exception. Thing was I'd met this ex-graphic designer who was quitting the rat race and going off to Zimbabwe and he was having a little farewell do in the flat of an air hostess friend of his in Mitcham, would I go? I thought, well it's not every day you get somebody going off to Zimbabwe, so I said 'Yes' and I'm glad I did because that's how I got the audition.

Now my hobby is people. I collect people. So when I saw this interesting-looking man in the corner, next thing is I find myself talking to him. I said, 'You look an interesting person. I'm interested in interesting people. Hello'. He said, 'Hello'. I said, 'What do you do'? He said, 'I'm in films'. I said, 'Oh, that's interesting, anything in the pipeline'? He said, 'As a matter of fact, yes', and starts telling me about this project he's involved in making videos for the overseas market, targeted chiefly on West Germany. I said, 'Are you the producer'? He said, 'No, but I'm on the production side, the name's Spud'. I said, 'Spud! That's an interesting name, mine's Lesley'. He said, 'As it happens, Lesley, we've got a problem at the moment. Our main girl has had to drop out because her back's packed in. Are you an actress'? I said, 'Well, Spud, interesting that you should ask because as a matter of fact I am'. He said, 'Will you excuse me one moment, Lesley'? I said, 'Why, Spud, where are you going'? He said, 'I'm going to go away, Lesley, and make one phone call'.

It transpires the director is seeing possible replacements the very next day, at an address in West London. Spud said, 'It's interesting because I'm based in Ealing'. I said, 'Isn't that West London'? He said, 'It is. Where's your stamping ground'? I said, 'Bromley, for my sins'. He said, 'That's a far-ish cry. Why not bed down at my place'? I said, 'Thank you, kind sir, but I didn't fall off the Christmas tree yesterday'. He said, 'Lesley, I have a son studying hotel management and a daughter with one kidney. Besides, I've got my sister-in-law staying. She's come up for the Ideal Home Exhibition'.

The penny began to drop when I saw the tattoo. My experience of tattoos is that they're generally confined to the lower echelons, and when I saw his vest it had electrician written all over it. I never even saw the sister-in-law. Still traipsing round Olympia probably.

*Go to black.*

*Come up on Lesley in the same setting. Afternoon.*

I know something about personality. There's a chapter about it in this book I'm reading. It's by an American. They're the experts where personality is concerned, the Americans; they've got it down to a fine art. It makes a big thing of interviews so I was able to test it out.

The director's not very old, blue suit, tie loose, sleeves turned back. I put him down as a university type. Said his name was Simon, which I instantly committed to memory. (That's one of the points in the book: purpose and use of name.) He said, 'Forgive this crazy time'. I said, 'I'm sorry, Simon'? He said, 'Like 9.30 in the morning'. I said, 'Simon. The day begins when the day begins. You're the director'. He said, 'Yes, well. Can you tell me what you've done'?

I said, 'Where you may have seen me, Simon, is in *Tess*. Roman Polanski. I played Chloë'. 'I don't remember her', he said. 'Is she in the book'? I said, 'Book? This is *Tess*, Simon. Roman Polanski. Chloë was the one on the back of the farm cart wearing a shawl. The shawl was original nineteenth-century embroidery. All hand done.

Do you know Roman, Simon'? He said, 'Not personally, no'. I said, 'Physically he's quite small but we had a very good working relationship. Very open'. He said that was good, because Travis in the film was very open. I said, 'Travis? That's an interesting name, Simon'. He said, 'Yes. She's an interesting character, she spends most of the film on the deck of a yacht'. I said, 'Yacht? That's interesting, Simon. My brother-in-law has a small power boat berthed at Ipswich'. He said, 'Well! Snap'! I said, 'Yes, small world'! He said, 'In an ideal world, Lesley, I'd be happy to sit here chatting all day but I have a pretty tight schedule and, although I know it's only 9.30 in the morning, could I see you in your bra and panties'? I said, '9.30 in the morning, 10.30 at night, we're both professionals, Simon, but', I said, 'could we just put another bra on because if we don't you won't be able to tell my tits from goose-pimples'. He had to smile. That was another of the sections in the personality book: humour, usefulness of in breaking the ice.

When I'd got my things off he said, 'Well, you've passed the physical. Now the oral. Do you play chess'? I said, 'Chess, Simon? Do you mean the musical'? He said, 'No, the game'. I said, 'As a matter of fact, Simon, I don't. Is that a problem'? He said, 'Not if you water-ski. Travis is fundamentally an outdoor girl, but we thought it might be fun to make her an intellectual on the side'. I said, 'Well, Simon, I'm very happy to learn both chess and water-skiing, but could I make a suggestion? Reading generally indicates a studious temperament and I'm a very convincing reader', I said, 'because it's something I frequently do in real life'. I could tell he was impressed. And so I said, 'Another suggestion I could make would be to kit Travis out with some glasses. Spectacles, Simon. These days they're not unbecoming and if you put Travis in spectacles with something in paperback, that says it all'. He said, 'You've been most helpful'. I said, 'The paperback could be something about the environment or, if you want to maintain the water-skiing theme, something about water-skiing and the environment possibly. I mean, Lake Windermere'.

He was showing me out by this time but I said, 'One last thought, Simon, and that is a briefcase. Put Travis in a bikini and give her a briefcase and you get the best of every possible world'. He said, 'I'm most grateful. You've given me a lot of ideas'. I said, 'Goodbye, Simon. I hope we can work together'. The drill for saying goodbye is you take the person's hand and then put your other hand over theirs, clasp it warmly while at the same time looking into their eyes, smiling and reiterating their name. This lodges you in their mind apparently. So I did all that, only going downstairs I had another thought and I popped back. He was on the phone. 'You won't believe this', he was saying. I said, 'Don't hang up, Simon, only I just wanted to make it crystal clear that when I said briefcase I didn't mean the old-fashioned type ones, there are new briefcases now that open up and turn into a mini writing-desk. Being an up-to-the-minute girl, that would probably be the kind of briefcase Travis would have. She could be sitting in a wet bikini with a briefcase open on her knee. I've never seen that on screen so it would be some kind of first. Ciao, Simon. Take care'.

*Pause.*

That was last Friday. The book's got charts where you check your interview score. Mine was 75. Very good to excellent. Actually, I'm surprised they haven't telephoned.

*Go to black.*

*Come up on Lesley, who is now made up and her hair done, sitting in a small bleak room in her dressing-gown. Morning.*

You'd never think this frock wasn't made for me. I said to Scott, who's Wardrobe, 'She must be my double'. He said, 'No. You're hers. The stupid cow'.

Talk about last-minute, though. Eleven o'clock on Tuesday night I'm just wondering about having a run round with the dustette, six o'clock next morning I'm sitting in Lee-on-Solent in make-up. When the phone went telling me I'd got the part I assumed it was Simon. So I said, 'Hello Simon'. He said, 'Try Nigel'. So I said, 'Well, Nigel, can you tell Simon that I haven't let the grass grow under my feet. I now play a rudimentary game of chess'. He said, 'I don't care if you play a championship game of ice hockey, just don't get pregnant'.

It transpires the girl they'd slated to do the part had been living with a racing driver and of course the inevitable happened, kiddy on the way. So my name was next out of the hat. I said to Scott, 'I know why. They knew I had ideas about the part'. He said, 'They knew you had a

38-inch bust'. His mother's confined to a wheelchair, he's got a lot on his plate.

Anyway, I'm ready. I've been ready since yesterday morning. It was long enough before anybody came near. I had a bacon sandwich which Scott went and fetched for me while I was under the dryer. I said, 'Wasn't there a croissant'? He said, 'In Lee-on-Solent'? On *Tess* there were croissants. On *Tess* there was filter coffee. There was also some liaison.

I wanted to talk to somebody about the part, only Scott said they were out in the speed boat doing mute shots of the coastline. On *Tess* you were never sitting around. Roman anticipated every eventuality. We filmed in the middle of a forest once and the toilet arrangements were immaculate. There was also provision for a calorie-controlled diet. I said to Scott, 'I'm not used to working like this'. He said, 'Let's face it, dear. You're not used to working. Why didn't you bring your knitting'? I said, 'I do not knit, Scott'. He said, 'Well, file your nails then, pluck an eyebrow, be like me, do something constructive'. He's as thin as a rail and apparently an accomplished pianist and he seems to be make-up as well as wardrobe. On *Tess* we had three caravans for make-up alone.

Eventually Simon puts his head round the door. I said, 'Hello, Simon'. I said, 'Long time no see. Did Nigel tell you I've learned chess'? He said, 'Chess? Aren't you the one who can water-ski'? I said 'No'. He said 'Bugger' and disappeared. I said to Scott, 'Simon's on the young side for a director'. He said, 'Director? He couldn't direct you to the end of the street. He just does all the running about'. I said, 'Who is the director'? He said, 'Gunther'. I said, 'Gunther? That sounds a continental name'. He said, 'Yes. German'. I said, 'That's interesting. I went to Germany once. Dusseldorf'. He said, 'Well, you'll have a lot to talk about'. I've a feeling Scott may be gay. I normally like them only I think he's one of the ones it's turned bitter.

I'm still sitting there hours later when this other young fellow comes in. I said, 'Gunther'? He said, 'Nigel'. I said, 'We spoke on the phone'. He said, 'Yes. I'm about to commit suicide. I've just been told. You don't water-ski'. I said, 'Nigel. I could learn. I picked up the skateboard in five minutes'. He said, 'Precious. Five minutes is what we do not have. You don't by any chance have fluent French'? I said, 'No, why'? He said, 'They'd wondered about making her French'. I said, 'Nigel. How can she be French when she's called Travis? Travis isn't a French name'. He said, 'The name isn't important'. I said, 'It is to me. It's all I've got to build on'. He said, 'I'll get back to you'. I said, 'Nigel. I don't have French but what I do have is a smattering of Spanish, the legacy of several non-package type holidays on the Costa del Sol. Could Travis be half Spanish'? He said to Scott, 'We wanted someone with fluent French who could water-ski. What have we got? Someone with pidgin Spanish who plays chess'. Scott said, 'Well, don't tell me. I started off a landscape gardener'.

I was still waiting to be used in the afternoon which is when they did the water-skiing. Some girl from the local sub-aqua did it. She works part-time in the quayside restaurant where they all ate last night apparently. I saw her when she came in for make-up. Pleasant enough but didn't look a bit like me. I'm quite petite, only she was on the large side and whereas my hair is auburn hers was definitely ginger. I didn't say anything at the time but I thought if she's supposed to be me they'll be into big continuity problems so I thought I'd go in quest of the director and tell him. Nobody about on the yacht except a man who's dusting the camera. He said not to worry, the shot was p.o.v. water-skis so we'd only be seeing her elbow. I said, 'Will that work'? He said, 'Oh yes. You know, Cinema, the magic of'. Mind you, he said, if it was up to him personally, he'd rather see my elbow than hers any day. His name was Terry, what was mine? I said, 'It's a relief to find someone civil'. He said, 'It's the usual story, Lesley, Art comes in at the door, manners go out of the window. Why is making a film like being a mushroom'?

I said, 'Why, Terry'? He said, 'They keep you in the dark and every now and again somebody comes and throws a bucket of shit over you'. He laughed. I said, 'That's interesting, only Terry, they don't grow mushrooms like that now. It's all industrialised'. He said, 'You sound like a cultured person, what say we spend the evening exploring the delights of Lee-on-Solent'?

His room's nicer than mine. His bathroom's got a hair-dryer.

*Go to black.*

*Come up on Lesley now in a bikini and wrap. An anonymous hotel room. Evening.*

Please don't misunderstand me. I've no objection to taking my top off. But Travis as I was playing her wasn't the kind of girl who would take her top off. I said, 'I'm a professional, Nigel. Credit me with a little experience. It isn't Travis'.

I'd been sitting on the deck of the yacht all day as background while these two older men had what I presumed was a business discussion. One of them, who was covered in hair and had a real weight problem, was my boyfriend apparently. You knew he was my boyfriend because at an earlier juncture you'd seen him hit me across the face. Travis is supposed to be a good-time girl, though you never actually see me having a good time, just sat on this freezing cold deck plastering on the sun tan lotion. I said to Nigel, 'I don't know whether the cameraman's spotted it, Nigel, but would I be sunbathing? There's no sun'. Nigel said, 'No sun is favourite'. Nigel's first assistant, here there and everywhere. Gunther never speaks, not to me anyway. Just stands behind the camera with a little cap on. Not a patch on Roman. Roman had a smile for everybody.

Anyway, I'm sitting there as background and I say to Nigel, 'Nigel, am I right in thinking I'm a denizen of the cocktail belt'? He said, 'Why'? a bit guardedly. I said, 'Because to me, Nigel, that implies a cigarette-holder', and I produced quite a modest one I happened to have brought with me. He went and spoke to Gunther, only Gunther ruled there was to be no smoking. I said, 'On grounds of health'? Nigel said, 'No. On grounds of it making continuity a bugger'. I'd also brought a paperback with me just to make it easier for props (which seemed to be Scott again). Only I'd hardly got it open when Nigel relieved me of it and said they were going for the sun tan lotion. I said, 'Nigel, I don't think the two are incompatible. I can apply sun tan lotion and read at the same time. That is what professionalism means'. He checked with Gunther again and he came back and said, 'Forget the book. Sun tan lotion is favourite'. I said, 'Can I ask you something else'? He said, 'Go on'. I said, 'What is my boyfriend discussing'? He said, 'Business'. I said, 'Nigel. Would I be right in thinking it's a drugs deal'? He said, 'Does it matter'? I said, 'It matters to me. It matters to Travis. It helps my character'. He said, 'What would help your character is if you took your bikini top off. I said, 'Nigel. Would Travis do that'? I said, 'We know Travis plays chess. She also reads. Is Travis the type to go topless'? He said, 'Listen. Who do you think you're playing, Emily Brontë? Gunther wants to see your knockers'.

I didn't even look at him. I just took my top off without a word and applied sun tan lotion with all the contempt I could muster. They did the shot, then Nigel came over and said Gunther liked that and if I could give him a whisker more sensuality it might be worth a close-up. So we did it again and then Nigel came over and said Gunther was liking what I was giving them and in this next shot would I slip off my bikini bottom. I said, 'Nigel. Trust me. Travis would not do that'. Talks to Gunther. Comes back. Says Gunther agrees with me. The real Travis wouldn't. But by displaying herself naked before her boyfriend's business associate she is showing her contempt for his whole way of life. I said, 'Nigel. At last Gunther is giving me something I can relate to'. He says, 'Right! Let's shoot it! Elbow the bikini bottom'!

*Pause.*

We wrapped about six (that's film parlance for packed up). I said to Nigel, 'Did I give Gunther what he wanted? Is he happy'? He said, 'Gunther is an artist, Lesley. He's never happy. But as he said this afternoon, "At last we're cooking with gas" '. I said, 'Does that mean it's good'? He said, 'Yes'. I said, 'Oh. Because I prefer electricity'.

When I got back to the hotel, it took me some time to unwind. I'd become so identified with Travis it was only when I'd had a bath and freshened up I felt her loosening her hold on me. I was looking forward to relaxing with the crew, swapping anecdotes of the day's shooting in the knowledge of a day's work well done only when I got downstairs there was nobody about, just Scott and one of the drivers. Turns out all the rest of them had gone off to supper at the restaurant run by the fat girl who did the water-skiing.

I sat in the bar for a bit. Just one fellow in there. I said, 'My hobby is people, what do you do'? Lo and behold he's on the film too, the animal handler, Kenny. In charge of the cat. I said, 'That's interesting, Kenny. I didn't know there was going to be a cat. I love cats. I love dogs too, but I love cats'. He said, 'Would you care to see her? She's asleep on my bed'. I said, 'That's convenient'. He said, 'Lesley. Don't run away with that idea. I am wedded to my small charges'. So I go up and pal on with the cat a bit and Kenny tells me about all the animals he's handled, a zebra once, a seal, an alligator and umpteen ferrets. He has a trout there too in a tank. It was going to be caught later on in the film. Quite small, only they were going to shoot it in close-up so it would look bigger.

I sat on the bed and listened to him talk about animal behaviour. I said, 'Kenny, this is the kind of evening I like, two people just talking about something interesting'.

I woke up in the night and couldn't remember where I was. Then I saw the cat sitting there, watching the trout.

*Go to black.*

*Come up on Lesley back in her own flat and in her ordinary clothes. Dusk.*

When you've finished a shot on a film you have to wait and see whether there's what they call a hair in the gate. It's film parlance for the all clear. Thank God there wasn't because I couldn't have done it again. I'd created Travis and though it was her lover that got shot I felt it was the something in me that was Travis that had died.

My lover's name turned out to be Alfredo. That was my big line. 'Alfredo'! He was the head of some sort of crime syndicate only everybody in the yachting fraternity thought he was very respectable and to do with the building trade. One night while Alfredo and me were ashore at a building federation dinner and dance this young undercover policeman swims out to the yacht to search it in his underpants. However, as luck would have it Travis has a headache, so she and Alfredo return early from this ultra-respectable function with Alfredo in a towering rage. Originally I was down to say, 'I can't help it Alfredo, I have a headache', and we tried it once or twice only Gunther then thought it would be more convincing if my headache was so bad I couldn't actually speak and Alfredo just said, 'You and your headaches'. I said, 'If it's a migraine rather than a headache Travis probably wouldn't be able to speak', and Gunther said, 'Whatever you say'. It's wonderful, that moment, when you feel a director first begin to trust you and you can really start to build.

Anyway Travis and Alfredo come into the cabin where they find this young man behind the sofa in his underpants and Alfredo takes out his gun and says, 'How lucky lovely Travis had a headache and we had to leave our glittering reception. I was cross with her then but now my mood has changed. Offer the gentleman a drink, Travis. Then go and take your clothes off. There's nothing I like better than making love after killing a policeman. Ha ha'. I then retire to the next cabin while Alfredo taunts this bare young policeman and says he is going to kill him, but before he does so, he tells him about his drug-smuggling operation in every detail, the way criminals tend to do the minute they get somebody at gunpoint. When Travis comes back with no clothes on the young policeman is talking about the evil drugs do, all the young lives ruined and so on. Only I forgot to say that there'd been some dialogue earlier, when I was supposed to be snorkelling, about how Travis had a little brother, Craig, and how he'd got hooked on drugs and how I was heartbroken and determined to revenge myself on the culprits should I ever come across them.

So when the policeman is saying all this about the horror of drugs you can see it comes as a revelation to Travis that her lover is involved in drugs: she thinks it's just been ordinary crime and stealing electrical goods. Anyway very quietly, 'almost pensively' Gunther said, Travis picks up an underwater spear gun that happens to be on the sideboard. Nigel came over and said that ideally at this point Gunther would like to see a variety of emotions chase themselves across Travis's face as her affection for her lover, Alfredo, fights with the demands of her conscience and the memories of her little brother, Craig. You see my lover's fat finger tighten on the trigger as he gets ready to shoot the policeman, only just then I say his name very quietly, 'Alfredo'. He spins round. Travis fires the harpoon and you see the spear come out of his back, killing him, and also ruining his dinner jacket. They then follow that with a big close-up with blood and everything, and me with a single tear rolling down my cheek.

We did this in one take, which Nigel said was almost unique in the annals of filming. Only Scott has to chip in and say good job, as just having one dinner jacket was fairly unique as well. I couldn't have done it again anyway. I'd got nothing left. Except I suddenly had a flash of inspiration, the way you do when you've been to the end of the world and back, and I said to Nigel, 'Don't you think that Travis, drained of all emotion by the death of her lover, would perhaps cling on to the policeman whose life she has saved, and that they would celebrate his deliverance by having sexual intercourse there and then'?

Big debate. Gunther really liked it, only the actor playing the policeman wasn't keen. I think he may have been gay too, he had a moustache. Eventually Nigel came over and said that favourite was for the policeman to look as if he was considering having sexual intercourse and for him to run his hand speculatively over Travis's private parts, only then pity drives out lust and instead he covers up her nakedness with an oriental-type dressing-gown, the property of her dead lover. Though even at this late stage you can tell he's not ruled out the possibility because as he's fastening the dressing-gown his fingers linger over Travis's nipples. Afterwards Gunther explained that if there had been any proper funny business at this point it would have detracted from the final scene when after all the excitement the undercover policeman goes home to his regular girlfriend, who cooks him a hot snack and who's a librarian, and then the final scene is of them making love, the message being that sexual intercourse is better with someone you're in love with even though they are a bit homely and work in the county library than with someone like Travis who's just after a good time. As Gunther said to me that night, 'It's a very moral film only the tragedy is, people won't see it'. I said to him, I said, 'That's interesting because I saw it that way right from the start'.

When we were in bed I said, 'If only we could have done this before'. He said, 'Lesley. I make it a rule never to lay a finger on an actress until the whole thing's in the can'. I said, 'Gunther. There's no need to explain. We're both professionals. But Gunther', I said, 'can I ask you one question? Was I Travis? Were you pleased with my performance'? He said, 'Listen. If someone is a bad actress I can't sleep with her. So don't ask me if I was pleased with your performance. This is the proof'. He's a real artist is Gunther.

When I woke up in the morning he'd gone. I wandered down for some coffee only there was nobody from the unit about. I'd planned to say goodbye to everybody but they were off doing some establishing shots of the marina. Anyway, I went and bought a card with a sinking ship on it and put 'Goodbye, gang! See you at the première'! and left it at the desk.

As I came out with my bags Scott was just loading the laundry. I said, 'Ciao, Scott. It's been a pleasure working with you'. He said, 'You win some, you lose some'. I said, 'Now it's back to real life'. He said, 'Some of us never left it'. It's funny the way their clothes are always too small.

The film's coming out in West Germany initially, then Turkey possibly. Gunther says it'll make me quite famous. Well, I suppose I shall have to live with that. Only I'm not just going it sit here and wait for the phone to ring. No fear. I'm going to acquire another skill. Spoken Italian. Selling valuable oil paintings. Canoeing. You see, the more you have to offer as a person the better you are as an actress. Acting is really just giving.

*Fade.*

MURIEL: STEPHANIE COLE

# Soldiering On

*Muriel is a brisk, sensible woman in her late fifties. She is
in a tweed skirt and cardigan with a single row of pearls,
and we come on her settled in a corner of her comfortable
home. It is afternoon.*

It's a funny time, three o'clock, too late for lunch but a bit early for
tea. Besides, there were one or two brave souls who'd trekked all the
way from Wolverhampton; I couldn't risk giving them tea or we'd
have had a mutiny on our hands. And I think people like to be offered
something even if they don't actually eat it. One's first instinct was to
make a beeline for the freezer and rout out the inevitable quiche, but
I thought, 'Muriel, old girl, that's the coward's way out', so the upshot
was I stopped up till two in the morning trundling out a selection of
my old standards . . . chicken in a lemon sauce, beef en croute
from the old Colchester days (I thought of Jessie Marchant), and
bushels of assorted salads. As it happened it wasn't exactly a salady
day, quite crisp for April actually, however Mabel warmed up the
proceedings with one of her famous soups, conjured up out of thin
air, so we lived to fight another day. Nobody could quite put their
finger on the flavour, so I was able to go round saying, 'Have you
guessed the soup yet? and that broke the ice a bit. I don't know what
had got into Mabel but she'd gone mad and added a pinch of curry
and that foxed most people. It was cauliflower actually.

Still, it was a bit sticky at the start as these occasions generally are.
There were people there one didn't know from Adam (all the Massey-
Ferguson people for instance, completely unknown quantities to
me), and then lots of people I knew I should know and didn't. But
whenever I saw anyone looking lost I thought of Ralph and grabbed
hold of someone I did know and breezed up saying, 'This is Jocelyn.

She's at the Royal College of Art. I don't know your name but the odds are you're in agricultural machinery', and then left them to it. It was a case of light the blue touch paper and retire.

Knowing Ralph, of course, it was a real mixed bag. Several there from the Sports Council and quite a contingent from Tonbridge, some Friends of Norwich Cathedral and the Discharged Prisoners Aid Society, Madge and Perce whom we met on the *Mauretania* on our honeymoon, Donald and Joyce Bannerman who were actually en route for Abu Dhabi, then Donald bought a paper at Heathrow, saw the announcement and came straight down. And one sweet old man who'd come all the way over from Margate. He said, 'You won't remember me, Mrs Carpenter, but I'm a member of the criminal fraternity'. I shrieked. As the vicar said: Ralph touched life at many points.

The children magnificent, of course, or Giles at any rate. Luckily Margaret didn't appear. But Giles took off all the Household Brigade people on a tour of the garden while Pippa coped with some of the bigwigs from the City. 'I don't think you know George', I heard one of them say, 'George cracks the whip at Goodison, Brown'. Poor souls, they both of them deserved medals. And Crispin and Lucy angelic, Crispin popping in and out of people's legs reaching up to fill the glasses. I wanted them to have a rest. 'No', said Giles, 'let them do it. They adored their grandpa'. 'Adored him', said Pippa, 'like we all did'.

The church had been absolutely chocker and I'd managed not to blub until right at the finish when they struck up with 'I vow to thee my country'. And then I'd a hundred and one things to do so I was perfectly all right until I saw awful Angela Gillespie had made the mistake of talking to boring old Frank from the firm, and I heard the dreaded words 'fork-lift trucks' and thought how many times I used to have to shut Ralph up in similar circumstances, and the idea of shutting Ralph up at all set me off instantly and I had to nip into the pantry to staunch the flow, shortly to be followed by Mabel who'd just fallen over one of his old wellingtons and promptly gone into floods. So we had a good laugh and a good cry over that before powdering our noses and hurling ourselves back into the fray.

When everybody'd gone I'm just having five minutes in the chair before tackling the debris when Margaret comes plunging into the room. She said, 'What were all those people'? I said, 'It was a kind of party for Daddy'. She said, 'Why? Is he dead'? I said, 'You know he's dead'. She said, 'Who killed him'? I said, 'Don't be such a donkey. Come along and we'll find you a tablet'. Some of Ralph's medicine's still in the cupboard. Fat lot of good that did, I thought, and poured it down the lav. Then felt a bit choked.

Anyway the tablet did the trick. I heard her walking about at two in the morning but I didn't get up. Except then I had to get up anyway because it suddenly came to me, in all the excitement I'd completely forgotten to feed the dogs.

*Go to black.*

*Come up on Muriel sitting in an armchair. Evening.*

Everybody I run into says not to take any big decisions. I staggered into the Community Centre bearing Ralph's entire wardrobe which Angela Gillespie had nipped in smartish and earmarked for Muscular Dystrophy. Five minutes later, Brenda Bousfield had come knocking at the door on behalf of Cystic Fibrosis. Knives out straightaway, I practically had to separate them. In fact I did separate them in the end, the City suits to Angela and Brenda the tweeds. All lovely stuff. Beautiful dinner jacket from Hawes and Curtis, done for Giles if he hadn't got so fat. Mind you, he didn't want the ties either. Angela did. 'Lovely jumble', she said. 'How're you coping? Don't take any big decisions, one day at a time, I don't see any shoes'.

Actually I'd been silly and kept his shoes back. I loved his shoes. Always used to clean them. 'My shoeshine lady'. 'Whatever you do', Angela said, 'don't give them to Brenda. They're top-heavy on staff, their group, it's well known. It all goes on the admin. We can use shoes'.

I thought I'd go into the library and see if Miss Dunsmore could find me something on bereavement. That's something I learned from Ralph: plug into other people's experience, pool your resources. 'A new experience is like travelling through unknown country. But remember, others have taken this road before you, old girl, and left notes. So Question no. 1: Is there a map? Question no. 2: Am I taking advantage of all the information available? It doesn't matter if you're going to get married, commit a burglary or keep a guinea pig; efficiency is the proper collation of information'. Oh Ralph.

Miss Dunsmore did a reconnoitre round, but the only information she could come up with was a book about burial customs in Papua, New Guinea. I think even Ralph would draw the line at that. However, she thought the Health Centre did a pamphlet on bereavement. Miss Dunsmore said she wasn't offering this as consolation but apparently elephants go into mourning and so, very strangely, does the pike. So we chatted about that for a bit. Told me not to take any big decisions, and if I was throwing away any of his books could I steer them her way as she ran some sort of reading service for the disabled.

I dropped into the Health Centre and the receptionist said there was a pamphlet on death; they'd had some on the counter, only the tots kept taking them to scribble on, so they hadn't re-ordered. She said she'd skimmed through it and the gist of it was not to take any big decisions and to throw yourself into something. I said, 'You don't mean the canal'? She said, 'Come again'? Nobody expects you to make jokes. As I was going out she called me back and said did Ralph wear spectacles? Because if he did, not to throw away the old pairs as owing to cutbacks they'd started a spectacles recycling scheme.

Back at base Mabel said Margaret had been plonked on the chair in the passage all morning with her bag packed and her outside coat on, and for some reason wellington boots. Said the police were coming. We manhandled her upstairs, and after about seventeen goes I managed to smuggle in a tablet which did the trick and she'd just settled down for a little zizz when who should draw up at the door but Giles.

He'd cancelled all his appointments, eluded the guards at the office and just belted down the A12 because he suddenly thought I might need cheering up, bless him. He could always get round Mabel ever since he was little, so she agrees to hold the fort while he whisks me off to lunch at somewhere rather swish. I thought to myself, I hope you're watching, Ralph, you old rascal, and eating your words. Ralph and Giles never got on for more than five minutes whereas, it's funny, he was always dotty about Mags.

When eventually we get back, what with all the wine etc. (I mean pudding *and* cheese), I'm just longing to put my head down, but Giles cracks the whip and gets me to sign lots of papers. It turns out Ralph's left me very nicely off. What with the house and all his various holdings, one way and another I'm quite a rich lady. He's tied a bit up for Margaret, nothing specific for Giles, but he doesn't mind because of course he doesn't need any and when I go he'll get it all anyway. But what I do have is what Giles calls a liquidity problem, and the first item on the agenda is to give me some ready cash, hence the papers. Then something about buying a forest. Bit wary to start with, said, 'Can I not mull it'? and Giles said, 'Well you can, but the index is going down'. I said, 'What about Mr Sherlock'? Giles said, 'You know what lawyers are'. Wish old Ralph could have seen me, signing away. He never showed me any papers at all, whereas Giles took me through them and explained it all. I suppose it's a different generation. What he did do, which made me feel a tiny bit shifty, was to take away three or four of the best pictures, the two carriage clocks and a couple of other choice items. Said that when the sharks from the revenue came round to assess the stuff for estate duty these were just the items that would bump the figure up. I said, 'What about the inventory'? Giles said, 'I think we'll just drag our brogues on that one'. Apparently everybody does it. He's just going to keep the stuff under the bed at Sloane Street until the heat is off, then back they come.

Margaret still lying on the bed when I went upstairs. Asleep she looks quite presentable. Daddy's little girl. Not so little now, those great legs. But as Mabel says, 'It looks as if we're on the hospital trail again'. If she goes in, I could perhaps go to Siena. Except I've nobody to go with. One keeps forgetting that.

*Go to black.*

*Come up on Muriel sitting at a table writing letters.*
*Afternoon.*

It's not an ideal place, no one is saying it is. Even Giles doesn't say that. In fact it's a perfect example of one of those places they're always famously about to scrap. Started life as a workhouse probably, during the Napoleonic Wars, and *qua* building not displeasing. As someone weaned on Nikolaus Pevsner and practically a founder member of the National Trust I wouldn't alter a single brick. And as an arts centre first rate. As a museum of industrial archaeology . . . couldn't be bettered. Or as a craft centre, weaving, pottery, a shop-window where craftsmen and craftswomen could make and display their wares . . . absolutely ideal, the very place. But as a mental hospital . . . oh no, no, no, no, no.

The food, for instance. The food has to cross a courtyard—the kitchen is so far away for all I know it may have to cross a frontier. One toilet per floor . . . I just put my head round the door and wished I hadn't; no telephone that I could see and the beds so crammed together if you got out of one you'd be into another. Dreadful.

And of course I keep thinking of Ridgeways, the cup of tea, the matron's parlour and that immaculate lawn. It would break old Ralph's heart. But Ridgeways costs money. It always did. First of the month, beg to inform, respectfully submit, all very nice but £600 on the dot. And more. And more. And as Giles says, 'Mummy no can do. That kind of money we do not have'. Well we do, but it's all tied up.

And whereas in normal circumstances one would have fought tooth and nail to keep her in the private sector, just out of respect for Daddy, nowadays we are in what Giles calls a different ball game. And the old thing minds. Goodness, he minds. I wanted him to come with me today but just the idea of the place upsets him so much he won't even set foot in it. And actually I feel the same, but where is that going to get us? I thought of Ralph (as if I ever think of anybody else) and I thought, 'Come on, Muriel. You're a widow lady, you've got time on your hands, if anybody's in a position to roll their sleeves up it's you'. So today when I paid Mags a visit I got the name of the hospital secretary, almoner it used to be called in my day, and bearded him in his den. He did have a beard actually and looked pretty sorry for himself besides. It turns out he has to precept for absolutely everything down to the last toilet roll, and if he does have any brainwaves about improvements and can sell them to his own management committee, he's still at the mercy of the regional spending programme.

I asked about a table-tennis table. He said, 'My point exactly'. A table-tennis table would mean going cap in hand to Ipswich, which he's not anxious to do since the vegetable steamer's on its last legs. And on the rare occasions he does have a bit of latitude he finds his hands are tied by NUPE. Well, the upshot is I'm writing sheaves of letters to everybody I've ever heard of in an effort to plug the hospital into the coffee-morning circuit and get a support group started. What I'm saying is that mental illness is a scourge. It's also a mystery, can occur in the best-regulated families and nobody knows why. I mean, take us. Why have we been singled out? Loving parents. Perfectly normal childhood, then this.

When I went in this afternoon, Margaret was weaving a basket, and not making a bad stab at it really, all things considered. It's lucky I arrived when I did because she'd just got to the part where she had to integrate the handle with the main body and she was making a real pig's breakfast of it. So I got cracking and showed her the whys and wherefores and actually ended up making both handles. Which seemed to make her a lot happier. She's never been much good with her hands. Giles was a real wizard.

Apropos Giles there's a bit of a crisis with the funds apparently. Nothing serious. A chum's let him down. Didn't read the small print. Says it's nothing to worry about, though we may have to pull our horns in a bit further. So I said, 'All hands to the pumps. With all Daddy's contacts in the City why don't I start up a little catering business, executive lunches and the like? Good nursery food and lashings of it'. Giles not sure. Thought these days they wanted something a bit more nouvelle. I laughed, I said, 'Don't you believe it. Men are overgrown schoolboys, always were. Preached salad at Ralph for years and what good did it do'? Giles said, 'Small detail, Mum: what are you going to use for capital'? So that put the tin hat on that one. It's this bloody liquidity thing. It's funny I never heard Ralph mention it.

*Go to black.*

*Come up on Muriel in a bare unfurnished room. A suitcase open. A tea-chest. Afternoon.*

Job sorting out the one or two things I want to keep, though quite honestly I'm not sorry to see the back of most of it. I feel it puts me more in the same boat as Ralph. Lay not up for yourself treasures on earth type thing. The lilies of the field syndrome. Said this to the vicar who was looking round. He thought this was a healthy attitude and how much did I think the walnut sidetable might fetch, it would go so well in their hall. Huge marquee on the lawn. People trooping through the house, and Angela Gillespie never away. Said how horrid it must be to see people poking about among one's prized possessions. I said, 'Yes', but it isn't really. The person I do feel sorry for is Mabel, who's had it to polish all these years. Still, she was getting on like a house on fire with the auctioneer's men, who were all so careful and polite I'd have married any one of them on the spot. Angela beefing on about all the dealers being here, putting up the prices, I thought good job. Still, however much it all fetches it will only be a drop in the ocean.

At one point Angela got the Duttons in a corner and started telling the tale. Said Giles had always been a wrong 'un. I turned round and said she didn't know what she was talking about, it had been a genuine mistake. She said, 'Mistake? Hundreds of people losing their life savings a mistake'? I said, 'So why do you think I'm selling up'? She said, 'It wasn't your fault. Why should you suffer? That's what worries me, Muriel, it's not fair on you'. Fair on me or not it didn't stop her buying the corner cupboard. She's had her eye on it for years.

I suppose Giles has been a scamp. But I don't think he's been wicked. Just not very bright that's all. Still, Sloane Street is in Pippa's name so that's a blessing, and the school fees were covenanted for years ago so it's not all gloom. I sat under the chestnut tree while the sale was going on, and thought how none of this would have happened if Ralph hadn't died. Then I heard him say, 'Buck up, old girl', and went and gave a hand with the tea. I haven't told Margaret yet. Her fourteen-year-old psychiatrist thinks this may not be the moment. Sees some signs of improvement. Margaret brought him some tulips last week. Picked them from one of the hospital flowerbeds. I apologised and said I could give them some of our bulbs. He said not at all, it was a sign she was becoming more outgoing. Wanted to know about Ralph and Margaret. I said, 'In what way'? He said, 'No particular way. When she was little'. I said, 'Ralph was fond of her: she was his little girl'. He said, 'Yes'.

Took the dogs up the hill later on. They're next I suppose. Bloody psychiatrist.

*Go to black.*

*Come up on Muriel in a plain boarding-house room. Evening.*

Crack of dawn this morning I routed out my trusty green cossy and spent a happy half-hour breasting the billows. The old cossy's seen better days and the moth has got into the bust but as the only people about were one or two brave souls walking the dog I didn't frighten the troops.

Came back hungry as a hunter so boiled myself an egg on the ring and had it with a slice of Ryvita, sitting in the window. Sun just catches it for an hour then, lovely. I tidied the room, did one or two jobs, and then toddled along to the library and had a walk round Boot's by which time it was getting on for lunchtime, it's surprising how time does go. When I think of the things I used to get through in the old days I wonder how I did it.

Been here about a month now. Got onto it via an advert in *The Lady*. Sledmere it's called, 'Holiday flatlets'. Off season, of course, and quite reasonable. I haven't quite got the town sorted out yet. I feel sure there must be a community here if only I can put my finger on it. I had a word with a young woman at the Town Hall. Blue fingernails but civil enough otherwise. Said was I interested in Meals on Wheels. I said, 'Rather. I was 2 i/c Meals on Wheels for the whole of Sudbury', a fund of experience. Brawn not too good but brains available to be picked at any time. She looked a bit blank. Turns out she meant did I want to be on the receiving end. I said, 'Not on your life'. But message received and understood. The old girl's past it. Hence the swim, I suppose.

Still, I soldier on and it's not quite orphans of the storm time. I look round the shops quite a bit and if I'm lucky I run into Angela Gillespie who's got her mother in a home here and comes over from time to time. We have coffee and a natter about the old days. Though I can't do that too often. Morning coffee these days seems to cost a king's ransom. And with me there doesn't have to be coffee. I can talk to anybody. The other morning I got chatting to one of these young men in orange who bang their tambourines in the precinct. Came up to me rattling his bowl, shaven head but otherwise quite sensible. His view is that life is some kind of prep. Trial run. Thinks we're being buffed up for a better role next time. As sensible as anything else I suppose. I said, 'Well, I just hope it's not in Hunstanton'. (*She laughs*).

The big bright spot on the horizon is Margaret. Heaps better, lost a lot of weight, got rid of that terrible cardigan and now is quite a good-looking young woman. In a hostel up to pres. but planning on getting a small flat. Came down last week and says next time it could be under her own steam, takes her driving test in ten days. Miracle. She took me out to lunch just like a normal girl. Talked about Ralph etc. Doesn't blame him, wishes he were alive. I don't know what I think.

Sorry for him, I suppose. She paid the bill and left a tip, just as if she'd been doing it all her life. Of course she'll be nicely off now, Ralph tied it all up so tight even Giles couldn't get his hands on it, the rascal.

Don't see him and Pippa much, not a peep out of them for over a month now. Doesn't like to come down, says it upsets him. Don't know why. Doesn't upset me. Miss the tinies. Not so tiny, Lucy'll be twelve now. And twelve is like fifteen. Married next. I'd seen myself as a model grandmother, taking them to Peter Pan and the Science Museum. Not to be. Another dream bites the dust.

My big passion now is the telly box. Never bothered with it before. These days I watch it all the time. And I'm not the discerning viewer. No fear. Rubbish. Australian series in the afternoons, everything. Glued to it all. Fan.

*The dialogue is more broken up now.*

I sometimes wonder if I killed Ralph. All those death-dealing breakfasts. We haven't had much weather to speak of. Eat less now. A buttered scone goes a long way.

*She picks up a Walkman and headphones.*

This is my new toy. Seen children with them, never appreciated what they were. Asked a young man for a listen in the precinct. Revelation. Saved up and bought one. Get the cassettes out of the library. Worth its weight in gold. Marvellous.

*She puts it on and henceforth speaks in bursts and too loudly.*

I wouldn't want you to think this was a tragic story.

*Pause.*

I'm not a tragic woman.

*Pause.*

I'm not that type.

*Fade out to the faint sound of the music, possibly Johann Strauss.*

DORIS: THORA HIRD
POLICEMAN: STEVEN BEARD

# A Cream Cracker Under the Settee

*Doris is in her seventies and the play is set in the living-room and hallway of her semi-detached house. She is sitting slightly awkwardly on a low chair and rubbing her leg. Morning.*

It's such a silly thing to have done.

*Pause.*

I should never have tried to dust. Zulema says to me every time she comes, 'Doris. Do not attempt to dust. The dusting is my department. That's what the council pay me for. You are now a lady of leisure. Your dusting days are over'. Which would be all right provided she did dust. But Zulema doesn't dust. She half-dusts. I know when a place isn't clean.

When she's going she says, 'Doris. I don't want to hear that you've been touching the Ewbank. The Ewbank is out of bounds'. I said, 'I could just run round with it now and again'. She said, 'You can't run anywhere. You're on trial here'. I said, 'What for'? She said, 'For being on your own. For not behaving sensibly. For not acting like a woman of seventy-five who has a pacemaker and dizzy spells and doesn't have the sense she was born with'. I said, 'Yes, Zulema'.

She says, 'What you don't understand, Doris, is that I am the only person that stands between you and Stafford House. I have to report on you. The Welfare say to me every time, "Well, Zulema, how is she coping? Wouldn't she be better off in Stafford House" '? I said, 'They don't put people in Stafford House just for running round with the Ewbank'. 'No', she says. 'They bend over backwards to keep you in your own home. But, Doris, you've got to meet them half-way. You're seventy-five. Pull your horns in. You don't have to swill the flags. You don't have to clean the bath. Let the dirt wait. It won't kill you. I'm here every week'.

149

I was glad when she'd gone, dictating. I sat for a bit looking up at me and Wilfred on the wedding photo. And I thought, 'Well, Zulema, I bet you haven't dusted the top of that'. I used to be able to reach only I can't now. So I got the buffet and climbed up. And she hadn't. Thick with dust. Home help. Home hindrance. You're better off doing it yourself. And I was just wiping it over when, oh hell, the flaming buffet went over.

*Pause.*

You feel such a fool. I can just hear Zulema. 'Well, Doris, I did tell you'. Only I think I'm all right. My leg's a bit numb but I've managed to get back on the chair. I'm just going to sit and come round a bit. Shakes you up, a fall.

*Pause.*

Shan't let on I was dusting.

*She shoves the duster down the side of the chair.*

Dusting is forbidden.

*She looks down at the wedding photo on the floor.*

Cracked the photo. We're cracked, Wilfred.

*Pause.*

The gate's open again. I thought it had blown shut, only now it's blown open. Bang bang bang all morning, it'll be bang bang bang all afternoon.

Dogs coming in, all sorts. You see Zulema should have closed that, only she didn't.

*Pause.*

The sneck's loose, that's the root cause of it. It's wanted doing for years. I kept saying to Wilfred, 'When are you going to get round to that gate'? But oh no. It was always the same refrain. 'Don't worry, Mother. I've got it on my list'. I never saw no list. He had no list. I was the one with the list. He'd no system at all, Wilfred. 'When I get a minute, Doris'. Well, he's got a minute now, bless him.

*Pause.*

Feels funny this leg. Not there.

*Pause.*

Some leaves coming down now. I could do with trees if they didn't
have leaves, going up and down the path. Zulema won't touch them.
Says if I want leaves swept I've to contact the Parks Department.
I wouldn't care if they were my leaves. They're not my leaves.
They're next-door's leaves. We don't have any leaves. I know that for
a fact. We've only got the one little bush and it's an evergreen, so I'm
certain they're not my leaves. Only other folks won't know that. They
see the bush and they see the path and they think, 'Them's her
leaves'. Well, they're not.
I ought to put a note on the gate. 'Not my leaves'. Not my leg
either, the way it feels. Gone to sleep.

*Pause.*

I didn't even want the bush, to be quite honest. We debated it for
long enough. I said, 'Dad. Is it a bush that will make a mess'? He said,
'Doris. Rest assured. This type of bush is very easy to follow', and
fetches out the catalogue. ' "This labour-saving variety is much
favoured by retired people". Anyway', he says, 'the garden is my
department'. Garden! It's only the size of a tablecloth. I said, 'Given a
choice, Wilfred, I'd have preferred concrete'. He said, 'Doris.
Concrete has no character'. I said, 'Never mind character, Wilfred,
where does hygiene come on the agenda'? With concrete you can feel
easy in your mind. But no. He had to have his little garden even if it
was only a bush. Well, he's got his little garden now. Only I bet that's
covered in leaves. Graves, gardens, everything's to follow.
I'll make a move in a minute. See if I can't put the kettle on. Come
on leg. Wake up.

*Go to black.*

*Come up on Doris sitting on the floor with her back to the
wall. The edge of a tiled fireplace also in shot.*

Fancy, there's a cream cracker under the settee. How long has that
been there? I can't think when I last had cream crackers. She's not
half done this place, Zulema.
I'm going to save that cream cracker and show it to her next time
she starts going on about Stafford House. I'll say, 'Don't Stafford
House me, lady. This cream cracker was under the settee. I've only
got to send this cream cracker to the Director of Social Services and

you'll be on the carpet. Same as the cream cracker. I'll be in Stafford House, Zulema, but you'll be in the Unemployment Exchange'. I'm en route for the window only I'm not making much headway. I'll bang on it. Alert somebody. Don't know who. Don't know anybody round here now. Folks opposite, I don't know them. Used to be the Marsdens. Mr and Mrs Marsden and Yvonne, the funny daughter. There for years. Here before we were, the Marsdens. Then he died, and she died, and Yvonne went away somewhere. A home, I expect.

Smartish woman after them. Worked at Wheatley and Whiteley, had a three-quarter-length coat. Used to fetch the envelopes round for the blind. Then she went and folks started to come and go. You lose track. I don't think they're married, half of them. You see all sorts. They come in the garden and behave like animals. I find the evidence in a morning.

*She picks up the photograph that has fallen from the wall.*

Now, Wilfred.

*Pause.*

I can nip this leg and nothing.

*Pause.*

Ought to have had a dog. Then it could have been barking of someone. Wilfred was always hankering after a dog. I wasn't keen. Hairs all up and down, then having to take it outside every five minutes. Wilfred said he would be prepared to undertake that responsibility. The dog would be his province. I said, 'Yes, and whose province would all the little hairs be'? I gave in in the finish, only I said it had to be on the small side. I didn't want one of them great lolloping, lamp post-smelling articles. And we never got one either. It was the growing mushrooms in the cellar saga all over again. He never got round to it. A kiddy'd've solved all that. Getting mad ideas. Like the fretwork, making toys and forts and whatnot. No end of money he was going to make. Then there was his phantom allotment. Oh, he was going to be coming home with leeks and spring cabbage and I don't know what. 'We can be self-sufficient in the vegetable department, Doris'. Never materialised. I was glad. It'd've meant muck somehow.

Hello. Somebody coming. Salvation.

*She cranes up towards the window.*

Young lad. Hello. Hello.

*She begins to wave.*

The cheeky monkey. He's spending a penny. Hey.

*She shouts.*

Hey. Get out. Go on. Clear off. You little demon. Would you credit it? Inside our gate. Broad daylight. The place'll stink.

*A pause as she realises what she has done.*

He wouldn't have known what to do anyway. Only a kiddy. The policeman comes past now and again. If I can catch him. Maybe the door's a better bet. If I can get there I can open it and wait while somebody comes past.

*She starts to heave herself up.*

This must be what they give them them frame things for.

*Go to black.*

*Come up on Doris sitting on the floor in the hall, her back against the front door, the letter-box above her head.*

This is where we had the pram. You couldn't get past for it. Proper prams then, springs and hoods. Big wheels. More like cars than prams. Not these fold-up jobs. You were proud of your pram. Wilfred spotted it in the *Evening Post.* I said, 'Don't let's jump the gun, Wilfred'. He said, 'At that price, Doris? This is the chance of a lifetime'.

*Pause.*

Comes under this door like a knife. I can't reach the lock. That's part of the Zulema regime. 'Lock it and put it on the chain, Doris. You never know who comes. It may not be a bona fide caller'. It never is a bona fide caller. I never get a bona fide caller.

Couple came round last week. Braying on the door. They weren't bona fide callers, they had a Bible. I didn't go. Only they opened the letter-box and started shouting about Jesus. 'Good news', they kept shouting. 'Good news'. They left the gate open, never mind good news. They ought to get their priorities right. They want learning that on their instruction course. Shouting about Jesus and leaving gates open. It's hypocrisy is that. It is in my book anyway. 'Love God and close all gates'.

*She closes her eyes. We hear some swift steps up the path and the letter-box opens as a leaflet comes through. Swift steps away again as she opens her eyes.*

Hello, hello.

*She bangs on the door behind her.*

Help. Help. Oh stink.

*She tries to reach the leaflet.*

What is it? Minicabs? 'Your roof repaired'?

*She gets the leaflet.*

'Grand carpet sale'. Carpet sales in chapels now. Else sikhs.

*She looks at the place where the pram was.*

I wanted him called John. The midwife said he wasn't fit to be called anything and had we any newspaper? Wilfred said, 'Oh yes. She saves newspaper. She saves shoeboxes as well'. I must have fallen asleep because when I woke up she'd gone. I wanted to see to him. Wrapping him in newspaper as if he was dirty. He wasn't dirty, little thing. I don't think Wilfred minded. A kiddy. It was the same as the allotment and the fretwork. Just a craze. He said, 'We're better off, Doris. Just the two of us'. It was then he started talking about getting a dog.

If it had lived I might have had grandchildren now. Wouldn't have been in this fix. Daughters are best. They don't migrate.

*Pause.*

I'm going to have to migrate or I'll catch my death.

*She nips her other leg.*

This one's going numb now.

*She picks up the photo.*

Come on, Dad. Come on, numby leg.

*Go to black.*

*Come up on Doris sitting with her back against the settee under which she spotted the cream cracker. It is getting dark.*

I've had this frock for years. A lame woman ran it up for me that lived down Tong Road. She made me a little jersey costume I used to wear with my tan court shoes. I think I've still got it somewhere. Upstairs. Put away. I've got umpteen pillowcases, some we got given when we were first married. Never used. And the blanket I knitted for the cot. All its little coats and hats.

*She puts her hand down.*

Here's this cream cracker.

*She rubs it.*

Naught wrong with it.

*She eats it.*

Making a lot of crumbs. Have to have a surreptitious go with the Ewbank. 'Doris. The Ewbank is out of bounds'. Out of bounds to her too, by the looks of it. A cream cracker under the settee. She wants reporting. Can't report her now. I've destroyed the evidence.

*Pause.*

I could put another one under, they'd never know. Except they might say it was me. 'Squatting biscuits under the settee, Doris. You're not fit to be on your own. You'd be better off in Stafford House'.

*Pause.*

We were always on our own, me and Wilfred. We weren't gregarious. We just weren't the gregarious type. He thought he was, but he wasn't.

Mix. I don't want to mix. Comes to the finish and they suddenly think you want to mix. I don't want to be stuck with a lot of old lasses. And they all smell of pee. And daft half of them, banging tambourines. You go daft there, there's nowhere else for you to go but daft. Wearing somebody else's frock. They even mix up your teeth. I am

H.A.P.P.Y. I am not H.A.P.P.Y. I am un-H.A.P.P.Y. Or I would be.

And Zulema says, 'You don't understand, Doris. You're not up to date. They have lockers, now. Flowerbeds. They have their hair done. They go on trips to Wharfedale'. I said, 'Yes. Smelling of pee'. She said, 'You're prejudiced, you'. I said, 'I am, where hygiene's concerned'.

When people were clean and the streets were clean and it was all clean and you could walk down the street and folks smiled and passed the time of day, I'd leave the door on the latch and go on to the end for some toffee, and when I came back Dad was home and the cloth was on and the plates out and we'd have our tea. Then we'd side the pots and I'd wash up while he read the paper and we'd eat the toffees and listen to the wireless all them years ago when we were first married and I was having the baby.

Doris and Wilfred. They don't get called Doris now. They don't get called Wilfred. Museum, names like that. That's what they're all called in Stafford House. Alice and Doris. Mabel and Gladys. Antiques. Keep them under lock and key. 'What's your name? Doris? Right. Pack your case. You belong in Stafford House'.

A home. Not me. No fear.

*She closes her eyes. A pause.*

POLICEMAN'S VOICE: Hello. Hello.

*Doris opens her eyes but doesn't speak.*

Are you all right?

*Pause.*

DORIS: No. I'm all right.

POLICEMAN: Are you sure?

DORIS: Yes.

POLICEMAN: Your light was off.

DORIS: I was having a nap.

POLICEMAN: Sorry. Take care.

*He goes.*